Gifts for Baby

Toys, Clothes & Nursery
Accents to Make with Love

Gifts for Baby

Toys, Clothes & Nursery Accents to Make with Love

Joanne O'Sullivan

LARK BOOKS

A Division of Sterling Publishing Company, Inc.

New York

ART DIRECTOR
Stacey Budge

PHOTOGRAPHER
Sandra Stambaugh

COVER DESIGNER
Barbara Zaretsky

COVER PHOTOGRAPHER
John Widman

ILLUSTRATORS
Orrin Lundrgen
Lorelei Buckley

PRODUCTION ASSISTANCE
Shannon Yokeley
Lorelei Buckley

EDITORIAL ASSISTANCE
Delores Gosnell
Helena Knox
Rain Newcomb

SPECIAL PHOTOGRAPHY
Sanoma Syndication
Peter Kooijman (pages 24, 40, 57)
Joss de Groot (page 29)
John Dummer (pages 58, 29)
Kees Rutten (page 82)
Freek Esser (pages 57, 93)
Dennis Brandsma (pages 25, 32, 53)
Rene Gonkel (pages 95, 96)

for maeve

Library of Congress Cataloging-in-Publication Data

O'Sullivan, Joanne.
  Gifts for baby: toys, clothes & nursery accents to make with love / by Joanne O'Sullivan.
    p. cm.
  ISBN 1-57990-366-5 (hard)
    1. Handicraft. 2. Infants' supplies. I. Title.

TT157 .O83 2002
745.5--dc21

2002028790

10 9 8 7 6 5 4 3 2 1

First Edition

Published by Lark Books, a division of
Sterling Publishing Co., Inc.
387 Park Avenue South, New York, N.Y. 10016

© 2003, Lark Books

Distributed in Canada by Sterling Publishing,
c/o Canadian Manda Group, One Atlantic Ave., Suite 105
Toronto, Ontario, Canada M6K 3E7

Distributed in the U.K. by Guild of Master Craftsman Publications Ltd., Castle Place, 166
High Street, Lewes, East Sussex, England
BN7 1XU
Tel: (+ 44) 1273 477374, Fax: (+ 44) 1273 478606, Email: pubs@thegmcgroup.com,
Web: www.gmcpublications.com

Distributed in Australia by Capricorn Link (Australia) Pty Ltd.,
P.O. Box 704, Windsor, NSW 2756 Australia

The written instructions, photographs, designs, patterns, and projects in this volume are intended for the personal use of the reader and may be reproduced for that purpose only. Any other use, especially commercial use, is forbidden under law without written permission of the copyright holder.

Every effort has been made to ensure that all the information in this book is accurate. However, due to differing conditions, tools, and individual skills, the publisher cannot be responsible for any injuries, losses, and other damages that may result from the use of the information in this book.

If you have questions or comments about this book, please contact:
Lark Books
67 Broadway
Asheville, NC 28801
(828) 236-9730

Manufactured In China

ISBN 1-57990-366-5

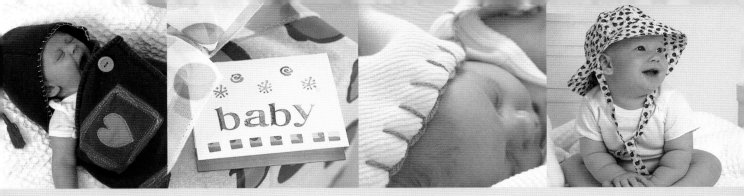

table of CONTENTS

introduction

A new baby brings joy that's contagious. It spreads from the parents-to-be to family and friends, filling everyone with anticipation and delight for months leading up to the big event. If you're reading this, you're likely to have caught it, and are looking for a way to create a meaningful and memorable gift for some special parents and their precious new arrival. Every baby gift is appreciated, but a handmade gift is a gift with heart—the perfect way to welcome a new baby to the world.

For generations and in cultures around the world, grandparents, cousins, friends, and neighbors have welcomed new babies with gifts made by their own hands. Although the materials or processes used may vary, the intention behind a handmade gift is universal and unchanged by time: to celebrate a new life, welcome a baby into a community or family, and express support for new parents as they begin their exciting journey into parenthood.

These days, it's easy to go into a store and choose a baby gift from a seemingly endless array of options. But now more than ever, a handmade gift is special. It says that you're willing to offer your talents and, just as important, your time, which is in such short supply nowadays. Whether your is gift is simple or elaborate, traditional or modern, practical or purely decorative, it will be remembered because it was made with care and love.

To make a special gift for Baby, you'll need inspiration and of course, instructions! That's what this book is here for.

In the first section of the book, you'll find tips and ideas to help you decide what gift to make. There's a guide to choosing materials especially for baby projects, and a sizing chart for babies up to one year old, as well as an introduction to basic stitches for non-sewers (if you already sew, think of it as a refresher course). Safety is a top priority for parents, so we've included some notes on making your gift safe for Baby.

Since first impressions count, there's a section on presentation and wrapping, featuring photos for inspiration. A gift isn't complete without a card, so we offer plenty of great ideas for making unique cards and gift tags, too. If you've ever wondered why baby boys wear pink and girls wear blue, or why the stork is said to deliver babies, you'll

find answers to those questions and more throughout the book in our Welcoming Babies columns which feature information on baby lore and traditions around the world.

Once you're ready to get started, turn to the project section for instructions, photos, and illustrations to help you make a gift you'll be proud to give. Whether you're a sewer or a general crafter, you're bound to find a project to match your skills and interests. The simple bookbinding, stamping, papier mâché, decoupage, and woodworking projects are easy and don't take a lot of time. A baby takes nine months to arrive, but making your gift doesn't have to take that long! Embellishing purchased items is a great shortcut to creating unique gifts, and we've provided plenty of ideas for transforming store-bought items into special handcrafted creations.

Parents and babies need a lot of supplies for the first year and beyond, including nursery items, travel accessories, clothes, and toys. We've got a sampling of projects from each of these categories, so you're sure to make a gift that parents will need and appreciate. Innovative design, interesting fabrics, and clever features distinguish these projects from the run-of-the-mill baby items you'll find in stores. These gifts are practical, too. The sewing projects feature modern, washable fabrics, and construction that will stand up to wear and tear from babies. Use our suggestions for materials, or choose your own and put your own personal stamp on the design.

Beyond the practical, there are projects that are fun, educational, and stimulating to Baby's developing senses. A mobile helps improve sight; balls, blocks, and rattles create wonderful sounds; soft toys are great for touch; a lavender sachet provides a soothing scent; and of course, there are bibs for taste! You can choose from gift ideas that are appropriate for Baby at different stages of development.

Last, but not least, these gifts are irresistibly cute! They're sure to warm the hearts of parents and make a long-lasting impression. A handmade gift will always be cherished because it was made with love!

baby gift
BASICS

CHOOSING YOUR GIFT

As the due date approaches, the excitement mounts for all those anticipating a new baby's arrival. Everyone wonders: Will the baby come in the middle of the night or in the taxi on the way to the hospital? How big will he be? Will he favor the father or the mother? And finally, what should I get for him? Everyone wants to let the new parents know that Baby will be welcomed and loved, but choosing the right gift can be tricky.

If you don't have children of your own, you may not know what parents really need. If your own kids are grown up, you may not remember what babies use at which age, or you may not be familiar with the newest trends in baby items. The following are some considerations to keep in mind when choosing your gift.

TRADITIONAL OR PRACTICAL?

When baby gifts come to mind, chances are the first thing you'll think of are the classic gifts that have been standbys for years: silver or pewter bowls, spoons, and rattles; delicate, airy linen christening gowns; and embroidered bonnets. These are the "gold standard" of baby gifts, imbued with a wonderful sense of tradition and nostalgia, and they're sure to be treasured by parents who receive them.

These days, however, many parents appreciate gifts that are more practical. Silver bowls and spoons are lovely to look at, but plastic ones are dishwasher safe! For most busy parents, a gift that's easy to use and care for will be remembered and valued for a long time. Gifts made of easy-care modern fabric, such as fleece or terry cloth, or gifts with multiple uses like the pillow on page 61 or the toy basket on page 62 will not only make an impression, but also receive a lot of use.

Time is also a factor to consider: a painstakingly crafted christening gown is a gift that can be handed down through the generations, but the demands of a busy modern schedule may leave you with little time to make one. Embellishing purchased clothing or nursery

WELCOMING BABIES

In many cultures, babies and families are given gifts of food. In Provence in southern France, a new baby was traditionally given salt, bread, an egg, and a match. The gifts represent the wish that the baby will grow *sage comme le sel de mer, bon comme le pain, plein comme un oeuf, et droit comme une allumette*— as wise as the salt of the sea, as good as bread, as robust as an egg, and as straight as a match. There is a similar tradition in Russia, and in Serbia, a new baby has traditionally received one grain of wheat, one coffee bean, one crystal of salt, a penknife, and a cross made of yew tree wood.

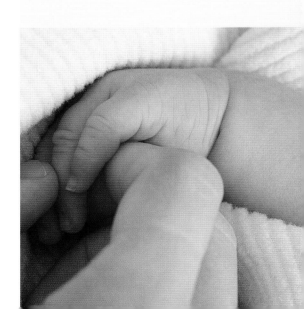

WELCOMING BABIES

Planting a tree to celebrate a baby's birth is a tradition that spans centuries and cultures around the world. In Switzerland and Germany, a pear tree was traditionally planted for a girl and an apple tree for a boy. In Israel, a cedar is planted for a boy and a cypress for a girl.

accents is a great alternative. Parents will appreciate that you created a special present for their baby.

Finally, consider a modern twist on one of the classics. A silver frame doesn't have to come from a jewelry store. The one on page 93 is made from papier mâché. If you don't have time to make a hand-embroidered linen gift, recycle a beautiful piece of vintage linen to make a new item, like the lavender sachet on page 54. Remember, it really is the thought that counts, not the time or money you spent making a gift.

NOW OR LATER?

With baby showers and visits from well-wishers, new parents end up with a lot of gifts, many of which they need and will use right away. But months down the road, when Baby's outgrown the newborn clothes, they may find themselves in need of different supplies for their ever-growing baby. Parents need different items at different times. Consider a gift with staying power. Blankets, pillows, and nursery accents can be used for a long time. If you decide to make clothing or toys, consider the following:

WHAT WILL BABY WEAR?

When new parents unwrap a beautiful handmade bunting, they may exclaim in delight, imagining their precious little bundle snuggled inside it. Seconds later, their delight may turn to disappointment when they realize that their baby will never, *ever* use it, since this bunting is sized for a two-month old, and their baby was born in July.

When making or buying clothes for a new baby, take out your calendar. You'll need to consider what size Baby will be during which season. Consider making an item that can be used a few seasons after the baby is born. If you're unsure about how large to make something, use the chart on page 16 as a guide. Baby clothes usually are sized in three-month intervals, and there's a lot of variation within each category. While each baby is different and standard sizes are only approximates, the chart will give you a general idea about size ranges.

Purchasing and embellishing premade clothes is a great solution to the baby size dilemma. You can get onesies or tops in 0 to 3, 3 to 6, and 6 to 9 month sizes so that Baby will have something special to wear at different times of the year.

WHICH TOY WHEN?

For the first few months of a baby's life, parents may try in vain to capture their baby's interest with a rattle or stuffed animal, while she seems content just to stare at their faces and smile. Mobiles are usually the first toy to fascinate Baby—since peripheral vision develops later, it's easier to view things that are in a straight line above her eyes.

As the months go on, Baby becomes more interested in colors, sounds, and movement, and toys that stimulate her first stages of growth are a great choice. Big soft toys that she can grasp and throw will help develop her motor skills, while rattles and other toys that make sounds can help her learn about cause-and-effect relationships: If I shake this, it makes a noise! Don't forget, however, that for much of the first year, a baby experiences most new things through his mouth. That's why toys made of soft, chewable material are a great idea (and another reason why machine washable toys are such a plus).

Above all, toys should be safe so that parents feel comfortable giving them to Baby. Toys that are commercially manufactured have to pass rigorous safety standards. Since you won't have the benefit of a safety inspector to check out your handmade gift, you'll need to be especially vigilant. Using small parts that can choke a baby or paint which isn't labeled as non-toxic isn't worth the risk. See the safety checklist on page 19 for more information.

IT'S A ..... BABY!
WHAT TO CHOOSE IF YOU DON'T
KNOW THE BABY'S GENDER

These days parents can find out the gender of their baby almost as soon as they find out they're expecting. While many jump at the chance to know, many parents-to-be still prefer to find out the gender when the doctor or midwife shouts "It's a girl!" or "It's a boy!"

If you don't know the gender of the baby who'll be receiving your gift, don't be discouraged—you still have a lot of options. Nursery accessories such as mobiles, organizers, blankets, bookends, toy chests, and crib sheets are perfectly wonderful gifts, and can be perfectly gender neutral. Parents of a baby of either gender will need diaper bag accessories and bibs, as well as towels and washcloths for bath time. Keepsake boxes, photo and memory albums, and frames are more ideas for great gifts that don't need to be gender specific.

Activity toys and stuffed animals are always a safe choice. While an eight-year-old boy may deny that he was ever deeply attached to his stuffed bunny, his parents will attest to the fact that it got lots of attention in his early years.

You can even give clothes with confidence. Just avoid pink and blue, and choose bright, vibrant colors—primaries like bold blue, green and red or bright oranges and purples, or sophisticated neutrals like sage or buttercup yellow. And don't forget—you can't go wrong with white. Both boys and girls can use buntings, hats, booties, sweaters, pants, blanket sleepers, and overalls. As you're making your gift, try to picture a baby of either gender wearing it. If you have any doubts, ask for a second opinion from a parent, especially one who has children of both genders.

A WORD ON SEWING FOR BABIES

Sewing and decorating clothing for children is part of a long, loving tradition among mothers, grandmothers, relatives, and friends of a new baby. Modern sewers may use different fabrics and embellishments, but their intention is still the same: to express their love, and welcome a baby into the community. When making special garments for these special little people, there are a few considerations to keep in mind.

FABRICS

You can't go wrong with soft fabrics—babies love to touch and taste them. We've used terry cloth, fleece, felt, faux fur, and soft cottons for many projects. When making toys, look for sturdy, tightly woven (but flexible) fabrics that don't fray. Terry cloth, and French terry cloth in particular, is wonderful for baby toys and clothes because of its soft and absorbent nature. Felt is great for toys because it's flexible and easy to shape and mold. Just make sure you use high-quality felt. Hold a piece up to the light—if you can see through it, it's too lightweight to be used.

Parents want clothes that are easy to wash, so your fabric also should be colorfast to stand up to frequent laundering. Always prewash fabrics before beginning to sew, not just to preshrink them, but to remove chemicals which may be present on the fabric and harmful to Baby.

STUFFING

Polyester fiber stuffing is a great choice for baby soft toys. It's washable and doesn't lump like some natural fiber stuffing. You can pack it tightly or loosely, depending on your project. Polyester fiber stays soft so toys will too.

THREAD

Use embroidery floss or quilting thread for durability when you're making toys or other items that must stand up to frequent use.

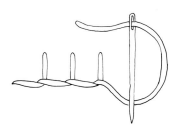

BLANKET STITCH

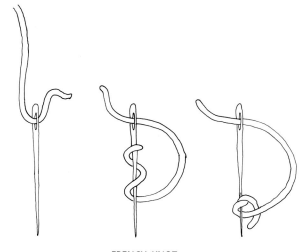

FRENCH KNOT

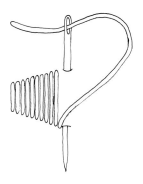

SATIN STITCH

BASIC STITCHES

If you sew, you're probably already familiar with these basic stitches. Just as a reminder, and for those who don't sew, here's a review of the stitches used in the projects in this book.

BLANKET STITCH

Working from left to right, bring the needle out to your edge or hem. Make an upright stitch to the right with the needle pointed down. Catch the thread under the point of the needle as you come out on the hem or edge. Repeat.

FRENCH KNOT

Twist the thread around the needle toward the tip. Sew into your fabric, then pull the thread to tighten. Sew back into the fabric next to the first hole. Pull the thread to knot.

SATIN STITCH

This stitch is often used for covering fabric entirely with stitches, and in this book it is used for creating noses and mouths on toys. On the right side of your work, bring the needle up at the lower edge of the area you want to cover, and insert the needle directly across the area. Make each stitch touch the previous one.

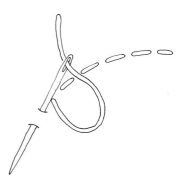

RUNNING STITCH

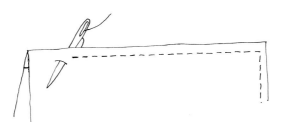

TOPSTITCH

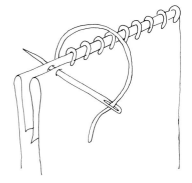

WHIPSTITCH

RUNNING STITCH

This is the simplest stitch and is often used for hand sewing. Bring the needle to the right side of your work and stitch from right to left.

TOPSTITCH

A topstitch is used on the right side of the fabric, about ¼ inch (6 mm) in from the edge. It's essentially the same as a running stitch and is used for decorative purposes when the stitching is a feature of the design.

WHIPSTITCH

Insert the needle into the fabric, then bring the needle and thread over the fabric edge. Insert the needle again ¼ inch (6mm) to the right of the starting point and repeat the process. Used for a strong, secure bond.

A PERFECT FIT: BABY SIZING

If you're making clothing for a baby who is yet to arrive, you may be unsure about measurements. Babies come in all shapes and sizes and grow at different rates. Standard baby clothing is labeled according to age, but the size is actually determined by a baby's weight and length. These markers are tied to pediatricians' growth charts, which track growth according to percentiles. For example, an "average" three-month-old (a baby at the 50th percentile of growth) may weigh 11 pounds (4.9 k) and measure 22 inches (55.8 cm). There are, of course, many babies who measure above average. Most babies wear clothes sized 3 to 6 months beyond their actual age, so plan to make clothes a little larger than you think they ought to be. If what you make doesn't fit Baby now, it soon will. Use the chart below as guide to help you size.

STANDARD BABY SIZES

	Weight	Length	Chest	Head	Thigh
0 to 3 months	Up to 12 lbs. (5.4 k)	22 to 25 in. (55.9 to 63.5 cm)	16 in. (40.6 cm)	14 in. (35.6 cm)	5 to 10 in. (12.7 to 25.4 cm)
3 to 6 months	12 to17 lbs. (5.4 to 7.7 k)	25 to 28 in. (63.5 to 71.1 cm)	17 in. (43.2 cm)	15 in. (38.1 cm)	10 to 13 in. (25.4 to 33 cm)
6 to 12 months	18 to 22 lbs. (8.1 to 9.9 k)	28 to 31 in. (71.1 to 78.74 cm)	19 in. (48.3 cm)	16 in. (35.6 cm)	11 to 14 in. (27.9 to 35.6 cm)

PRESENTING YOUR GIFT

A handmade gift that's thoughtfully designed and lovingly made deserves special packaging, too. Take the time to wrap and present your gift with care. Your goal is simplicity and style, and a package that looks as sweet on the outside as the special gift on the inside.

If you don't know the baby's gender, use wrapping paper or bags with polka dots, plaids, or neutral colors like yellow and green. Layers and layers of tissue paper add dimension and color. Baskets also make a great presentation and are bound to be useful to new parents.

For ties and ribbons, use innovative materials such as pipe cleaners or craft foam, or use raffia or other natural materials. Attach a beautiful length of vintage children's ribbon or trim to the package. Incorporate vintage photographs, or photographs of the baby's parents when they were children. Diaper pins stuck through ribbon are a clever touch, and may even end up being useful!

Consider adding another little gift to the package, tied to the ribbon. Rattles, charms, or small, inexpensive stuffed animals are delightful extras to add to a gift wrap.

Make a special handmade card or gift tag to top it off (see page 18 for ideas). A specially wrapped package will make a wonderful impression on the parents-to-be and express how much the new baby means to you.

SPECIAL DELIVERY: GIFT TAGS AND CARDS

Charming handmade tags can transform the image of a gift, and they're surprisingly easy to make. Plain cardstock tags are very inexpensive and available at most office supply stores. Look for rubber stamps with vintage images of children or babies, and stamp the images on the tags using soft-colored inks. You can layer your stamped images (see photo below) to add wings or halos. Create a collage on your tag using strips of beautiful handmade paper. If you're a stamp collector or know where to find vintage stamps, look for a "special delivery" stamp to add to your tag—it's the perfect embellishment for a baby gift tag. Attach a pretty silk ribbon to the tag for a finished look.

For beautiful baby cards, keep in mind two design principles: texture and dimension. Start with a cutout shape of very simple, recognizable image (a few ideas are shown above, but you could also try an umbrella for a baby shower, a baby carriage, or even a simple 'B' for Baby). Add a layer of fabric behind your image for texture. Faux fur and fleece are one way to go, or you could create a more nostalgic feel with gingham, lace, or a sweet cotton print. You can fashion a simple image from wire to add dimension to your card, and add beads with strong glue. Using any kind of hole punch or die cut will give your card a layered look, too. Finally, insert your card in a glassine or vellum envelope (available at stationery stores) so that your hard work and creativity won't be hidden behind a conventional paper envelope.

ABOVE: Large cards by Nicole Tuggle, small cards by Luann Udell
LEFT: Gift tags and card by Luann Udell

SAFE BABY, HAPPY PARENTS

Nothing is more important to parents than the safety of their children, so when designing a handmade gift for a child, always make safety a primary consideration. Chances are your attention to detail will result in a product much sturdier than any commercially made item available. Just to be sure, however, keep the following points in mind.

The item should be a safe size. Tiny babies have tiny mouths that they love to fill with anything they can get ahold of. To safeguard against choking, make toys or toy parts larger than ⅝ inch (15.9 mm) in diameter. Rattles should be at least 1⅝ inches (4.1 cm) across.

The item should be well-constructed. Removable or breakable parts can cause myriad hazards for Baby. When you've finished making something, try to pull it apart yourself. If you can do it, Baby probably can, too—they're surprisingly strong and very determined! Babies find uses for things that you could never imagine. Remember that a baby will drop or throw a toy again, and again, and again, so whatever you make must be able to stand up to that kind of test. If you make something with buttons, make sure they're very securely attached with the sturdiest thread you can find. You can even reinforce the attachment with glue.

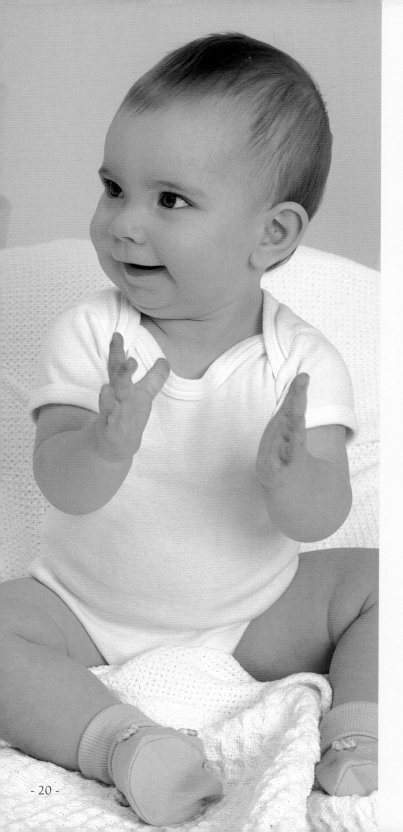

If an item is painted, make sure the finish is nontoxic. Everything a baby touches eventually ends up in his mouth, and when his teeth start to come in, a baby starts to gnaw and chew on everything he can. Seal painted surfaces as well as you can to avoid paint chipping.

Avoid long strings and cords and sharp edges. Ribbons, cord, or string shouldn't be more than 6 inches (15.2 cm) long. Anything longer could wind up around a baby's neck or trip him. If you use ribbons, make sure they are sewn securely to the toy or article of clothing. Don't make items with sharp edges that could poke or scratch the baby.

Can it be washed? Once again, the everything-goes-in-the-mouth factor comes into play. Parents need to wash toys and clothes frequently to avoid the germs that spread so rapidly among children. Choose materials that are easy to care for and clean. Prewash all fabrics before using them to set dye and remove chemicals.

the projects

BABIES LOVE BRIGHT COLORS

and simple shapes, and this flower garland combines both. It's great in a window, as shown here, or use it as a wall decoration to add color without the permanence of paint or wallpaper. This eye-catching accessory will fascinate Baby and stimulate her sense of sight.

FLOWER GARLAND

DESIGNER: TERRY TAYLOR

YOU WILL NEED
Nylon kite twine
Scissors
Measuring tape or ruler
Precut craft foam floral shapes*
Hot glue gun and glue sticks
2 pushpins

*You can cut out your own designs if you like.

1. Cut a length of twine 6 inches (15.2 cm) longer than the width of your window. If you don't know the size of the window, estimate that you'll need about 3 to 4 feet (91.44 cm to 1.2 m) of twine.

2. Lay a floral shape under your twine, about 2 inches (5.2 cm) in from the edge. Hot glue the twine and spread some hot glue on the shape as well. Lay an identical shape on top, sandwiching the twine. Press together the two shapes. Continue gluing flower shapes along the twine at evenly spaced intervals.

3. Cut additional lengths of twine longer than the length you cut in step 1. The garland in the picture is made of three lengths. Knot each length at both ends.

4. Use pushpins to tack the twine to a door or wall, then glue floral shapes to each additional piece of twine as you did in step 2. As you place flowers on the twine, you will be able to see how the garland hangs as you add flowers.

5. Knot additional lengths of twine to the garland as desired. Make your garland "grow" with more flower shapes.

WELCOMING BABIES

In the Orkney Islands (north of Scotland), fathers "wet the head" of their baby with whisky for good luck, then share the rest of the bottle with other men in the neighborhood.

heart-felt
BOOTIES

WHILE THESE BOOTIES *keep baby's feet toasty, the precious heart-shaped appliqués will warm the hearts of her parents. This project is simple but special. Try other motifs, too—stars, flowers, and crowns are easy to make and delightful to look at.*

YOU WILL NEED

Heart template on page 120
Scissors
Small squares of craft felt or denim
Fabric marker or pencil
Large-eye needle
Embroidery thread

1. Prewash booties.

2. Copy the heart template on page 120, reducing or enlarging it to fit on the top of the booties. Cut out the heart pattern, lay it on the felt, trace around it, and then cut out the shape.

3. Center the heart shape on top of the bootie. Using a simple running stitch, stitch the heart to the bootie. Knot the thread on the inside. Repeat for the other bootie.

BABY KIMONO TOP
with embroidered trim

THESE CUTE BABY TOPS *are called kimonos because they wrap around and tie on the side. Parents love them because they're easy to get on and off—no need to pull it over a wriggly baby's head. You can find plain white cotton kimono tops in any baby store and easily embellish them with simple, beautiful embroidery. The stitches are easy enough for beginners, so go ahead and make several tops in different patterns or colors.*

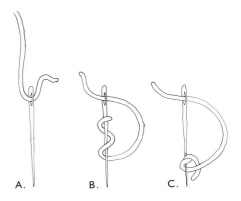

A.   B.   C.

FIGURE 1

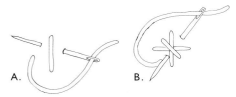

A.   B.

FIGURE 2

YOU WILL NEED
Prewashed purchased baby kimono top
Embroidery thread in contrasting colors
Embroidery needle
Scissors

1. Stitch a line of evenly spaced French knots (see figure 1) along the bound edge of the kimono top. In between each knot, run the thread inside the bound edge.

2. Stitch a three-legged stitch (see figure 2) between each French knot. Run the thread inside the bound edge between stitches.

3. Repeat the design all around the bound edge of the kimono.

big, fun, soft
BABY BLOCKS AND BALLS

DESIGNER: ALLISON SMITH

WHEN BABIES ARE LEARNING *early motor skills, big balls or blocks are great developmental toys. They can grasp, shake, and lift these toys, and even put them safely in their mouths. The bell stuffed inside sounds intriguing to Baby every time she shakes it. She'll want to discover it over and over again. You can make these delightful toys in no time with very simple sewing. Customize the fabrics to the taste of the parents, or just use bright colors that babies love.*

YOU WILL NEED
3 coordinating fabrics, 1 yard (91.4 cm) each
Template on page 113
Measuring tape
Scissors
Sewing machine
Coordinating thread
Iron
Large bells or other noisemakers
Polyester fiber filling
Sewing needle

FOR THE BLOCKS

1. The blocks can easily be made in different sizes: 6-inch (15.2 cm), 9-inch (22.9 cm), or 12-inch (30.5 cm) squares. Cut two squares of fabric in each of the three colors. You will have a total of six squares of fabric.

2. Arrange your fabric according to the diagram (see figure 1).

3. Sew sides C-A-C together with right sides facing. Press seams open.

4. Sew side A1-B together with right sides facing, then sew to C-A-C as shown in figure 1. Press seams open.

5. Sew side B1 on to the rest of the figure last with right sides facing.

6. Pin right sides together and sew.

7. Pin top A1 down, leaving a 2-inch (5.2 cm) opening for stuffing.

8. Trim the seams to ¼ inch (6 mm) and turn right side out.

9. Stuff the block with fiber stuffing, add a bell or other noisemaker, and whipstitch (see page 15) closed.

FOR THE BALL

1. Copy the template on page 113. Lay or pin the template on a piece of your first fabric and trace and cut around it. Cut two pieces of the first fabric. Repeat, cutting two pieces in each of the two additional contrasting fabrics.

2. With right sides facing, sew together two pieces in contrasting fabrics, leaving a ⅜-inch (9.5mm) seam allowance. Add an additional piece cut out of the third fabric. Repeating the same order of the pattern, sew together the additional three pieces. Trim the seams. Snip around the curves of the inside edges to relax the seams and press.

3. With right sides together, sew together the two three-piece panels of fabric. Leave a 2-inch (5.2 cm) opening for stuffing.

4. Turn the ball right side out. Stuff with polyester fiber stuffing. Add a bell and hand stitch the opening closed.

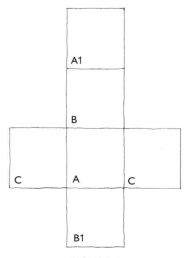

FIGURE I

WASHCLOTH AND TOWELS

BATH TIME IS A PERFECT TIME *to pamper Baby. Sweet-smelling soaps and bath lotions are relaxing, and warm, soft towels bundle him in comfort. This charming crown motif is the perfect embellishment for bath accessories for little princes and princesses. Washcloths and towels are easy to embellish and are a perfect gift when you don't know the baby's gender yet—every baby needs a bath!*

WELCOMING BABIES

In U.S. tradition, a father hands out cigars to friends after the birth of his child. It's not clear how this custom started, but some speculate that it's related to the Native American potlatch custom of smoking a pipe to celebrate various occasions.

YOU WILL NEED

Crown template on page 108
Scissors
2 washcloths in coordinating colors, or 1 washcloth and 1 towel in coordinating colors
Fabric marker or pencil
Thread in coordinating colors
Sewing machine

1. Copy the crown template on page 108, enlarging or reducing to fit your washcloth.

2. Choose the color for the crown motif. Fold the washcloth in that color in half. Center the template on the top fold and trace around it with the marker or pencil. Cut out the shape.

3. Fold the remaining washcloth or towel in half. Center the crown on the top fold. Serge or zigzag stitch the crown to the washcloth or towel.

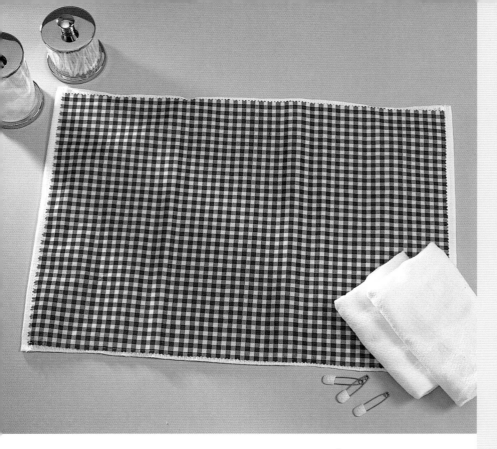

pretty and practical
PORTABLE CHANGING PAD

DESIGNER: JOAN MORRIS

A PORTABLE CHANGING PAD *is a must for any family on the go. This clever design is easy to make using oilcloth that wipes clean and a terry cloth towel that absorbs liquid. The pad rolls up to fit in a diaper bag or tuck into a backpack. You need only the most basic sewing skills to create it. The colorful oilcloth will complement any stylish diaper bag.*

YOU WILL NEED

½-yard (45.7 cm) of patterned oilcloth*

Pinking sheers

Hand towel in coordinating color

Thread in coordinating color

Scissors

Sewing machine

Measuring tape

Fabric marker or pencil

*You can also use vinyl or a premade tablecloth.

1. With pinking sheers, cut out oilcloth to fit ¼ inch (6 mm) in from the edge of the hand towel on all sides.

2. Place the oilcloth and hand towel together, back sides facing each other.

3. Starting at the short edges, machine stitch the two pieces together ¼ inch (6 mm) in from the edge.

4. Machine stitch the long edges together in the same manner.

5. Measure the pad into thirds and mark the measurement on each long edge. Machine stitch across from long edge to long edge at the marks you made. This reinforces the connection of the hand towel to the oilcloth so that the pad doesn't sag.

moon and stars

CRADLE SHEET

DESIGNER: TERRY TAYLOR

THE MOON AND STARS *are the perfect companions to escort Baby off to dreamland, so stamp her cradle or crib sheet with these charming celestial motifs. A plain white cradle sheet, rubber or foam stamps, and washable fabric paints are all you need. It's so easy to embellish a sheet that you may want to stamp several different ones with different images—flowers, butterflies, teddy bears, or hearts are just a few ideas to get you started.*

YOU WILL NEED
Fitted cradle or crib sheet
Newsprint
Foam brush
Bold rubber stamps
Fabric paints
Small paintbrush

1. Prewash your sheet.

2. Lay the fitted sheet face down on a flat surface. Place several flat layers of newsprint inside it. Push the layers out to protect the sides of the sheet from paint. Holding two corners, turn the sheet face up. Adjust the paper as needed.

3. Use a foam brush to apply one color of paint evenly on your stamp. Stamp the image with gentle and even pressure. If the color on the image is patchy, use the small paintbrush to touch up the color.

4. Set the fabric paint according to the manufacturer's instructions.

WELCOMING BABIES

In Cambodia, strings with money attached are tied around a baby's wrist as presents.

star bright

APPLIQUÉ TOP

PLAIN WHITE T-SHIRTS AND ONESIES *are a safe bet when you're buying for a new arrival and don't know the gender. But basic white can be boring. You can easily add interest with simple appliqués and basic hand stitching. The star motif is a great choice for girls or boys, but you could easily adapt the idea for other motifs, from a flower to a tugboat in silhouette.*

YOU WILL NEED

Star template on page 108

Scissors

2 small pieces of contrasting fabric*

Fusible webbing (optional)

Iron

Prewashed purchased shirt or onesie

Embroidery thread

Embroidery needle

Straight pins

Thread in coordinating color

Sewing needle

1. Copy the star template on page 108. Use the template to cut out a star shape from one of your fabrics. If your fabric is flimsy, cut the same shape from fusible webbing and attach it to the appliqué according to the manufacturer's instructions.

2. Cut out a rectangular shape somewhat larger than your star shape.

3. Thread the embroidery needle with three strands of embroidery thread. Use a simple running stitch (see page 15) to create the swirl on the star, starting from the innermost part of the swirl.

4. Pin the star shape to your fabric rectangle. Thread your needle with sewing thread. Hemstitch or whipstitch (see page 15) the star to the rectangle, turning under the raw edges of the star as you stitch.

5. Pin the rectangle to the shirt. Use a hemstitch or whipstitch to appliqué the rectangle to the front of the shirt.

6. Use your embroidery needle and embroidery thread to create a running stitch detail in the bound neck opening of the shirt.

WELCOMING BABIES

In Ancient Greece, parents placed a piece of woolen fabric over their door to report the birth of a baby girl. A wreath of olive branches was placed over the door to announce a boy's arrival. In Korean culture, a string of red peppers is hung outside a family's home to announce the arrival of a boy. If the new baby is a girl, parents hang straw and charcoal above the door. Once these items are displayed, it is the custom that well-wishers wait 21 days before visiting the mother and new baby.

beaded

BABY BOOTIES

DESIGNER: TERRY TAYLOR

BABY BOOTIES ARE A CLASSIC GIFT, *but not everyone has the time or skill to knit them. Beaded booties are a fast-and-easy alternative. Start with plain purchased booties and attach special beads in the colors of your choice. The designer chose a simple arrangement, but you may even want to trace a motif onto a bootie with a marker and use small seed beads to bead over it. These booties are best for small babies who haven't yet discovered that they can put their feet in their mouths!*

YOU WILL NEED

Booties

Large, decorative beads*

Nylon beading thread

Sewing needle

Scissors

*The designer used antique Czech beads on the booties. Use whatever beads you wish. Pretty novelty or mother-of-pearl buttons would look nice as well.

1. Thread your needle with a doubled length of beading thread. Knot the end of the thread.

2. Working from the inside to the outside of the bootie, bring the needle through, and make a backstitch (sew back and forth over your stitch a few times). Slip the bead onto the needle.

3. Pass the needle into the bootie. Make a line of small running stitches behind the area where the bead lies. Bring the needle to the outside and pass it back through the bead.

4. Pass the needle to the inside of the bootie, make a backstitch, and knot the end. Cut off the excess thread. Repeat for each bead.

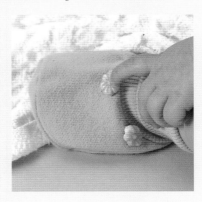

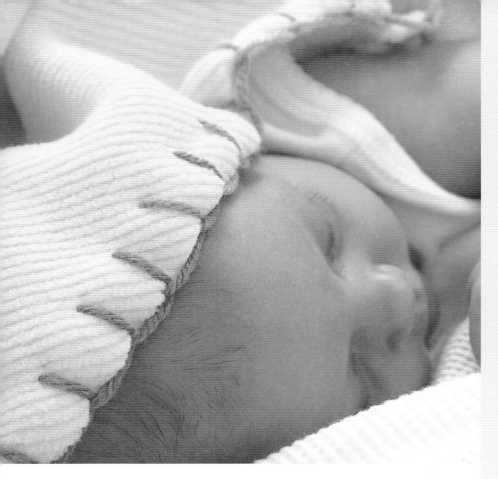

buttercup fleece
STROLLER BLANKET
DESIGNER: ALLISON SMITH

EVERY NEW BABY NEEDS *plenty of blankets, in different shapes, sizes, and weights. This soft, fleecy one is so easy to make that you don't even need a sewing machine. The round shape makes it perfect for strollers (it won't get caught in the wheels) or for playtime on the floor. Baby will love the soft texture and parents will love the clever design!*

YOU WILL NEED
Variegated colored yarn
Scissors
Fleece fabric, about 2 yards (1.8 m)
Measuring tape
Large piece of cardboard
Masking tape
Thumbtack
Fabric pencil
Large-eye embroidery needle

1. Decide how big you want your blanket to be. Make a large loop of yarn that is half the desired diameter of the project.

2. Unfold the fabric onto a flat surface. Place a piece of cardboard under the center of the fabric. Tape the cardboard down to the flat surface so that it doesn't shift.

3. Press the thumbtack through the cardboard into the center of the fabric. Wrap one end of the yarn loop around the tack and the other around the fabric pencil. Stretch the yarn out from the tack to pull open the slack, and trace a large circle on the fabric.

4. Cut out the circle.

5. Blanket stitch (see page 14) around the edge with the variegated yarn.

YOU WILL NEED

Prewashed snap tops or onesies

Newspaper

Small foam brush

Fabric paint

Bold graphic rubber stamps*

Unused pencil eraser

Small paintbrush

*You can use purchased stamps or make your own by gluing precut craft foam shapes onto small blocks of wood.

1. Be sure that your fabric is pre-washed. If you don't know, take the time to wash and dry the fabric.

2. Place newspaper underneath the top or between fabric layers.

3. Use the foam brush to spread fabric paint on the stamp. Don't overload the stamp.

4. Press the stamp onto the fabric with gentle, even pressure.

5. If needed, brush additional paint on the image with a small brush. Let the paint dry.

6. Decorate the neckline and front edge of the top with small dots. Use the pencil eraser as a rubber stamp.

one-of-a-kind

SNAP TOPS

DESIGNER: TERRY TAYLOR

PLAIN WHITE SNAP TOPS *are a staple of a baby's wardrobe. It's easy to add charm and personality to these practical cover-ups with rubber stamps and fabric paint. Buy a six-pack of tops and try different designs and colors on each, or personalize your gift by stamping on the baby's name or birth date.*

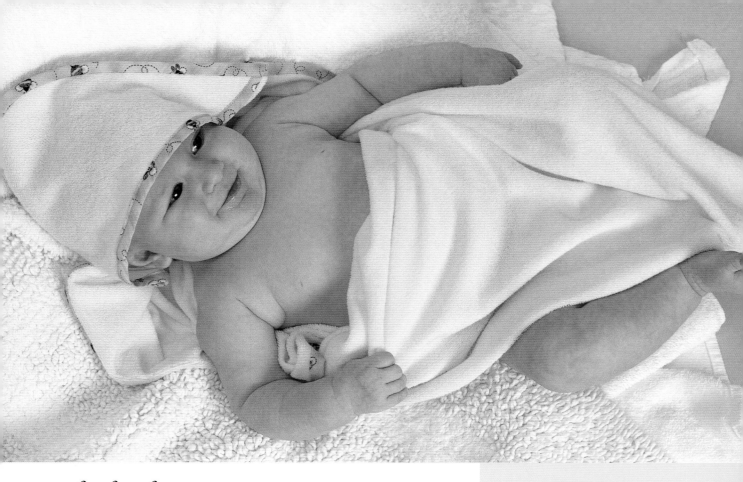

baby bee
HOODED BATH TOWEL
DESIGNER: JOAN MORRIS

ONE OF BABY'S FAVORITE TIMES *of day is bath time, and a wrap in a cozy hooded towel is a wonderful way to dry off. This one is made from French terry cloth, especially soft on baby's delicate skin. With very simple sewing, you can complete this project in a matter of hours. Personalize the colors, binding fabric, or appliqués to the parents' taste or the baby's gender.*

YOU WILL NEED
1 yard (91.44 cm) of French terry cloth
½ yard (45.72 cm) of print fabric
Scissors
Sewing machine
Iron
Pins
Sewing needle
Thread in coordinating color
2 bee appliqués
Invisible thread

1. Prewash the terry cloth and print fabric.

2. Cut a 34 x 34-inch (86.3 x 86.3 cm) square from the terry cloth.

3. Cut a 10 x 10 x 14-inch (25.4 x 25.4 x 35.6 cm) triangle from the terry cloth.

4. Cut seven ½-inch (1.2 cm) wide bias strips from the print fabric. Sew six of them together at the ends according to the diagram (see figure 1).

5. Press the remaining print fabric strip in half lengthwise. Press the raw edges into the center fold (see figure 2). Fold the strip over the 14-inch (25.4 cm) edge of the terry cloth triangle, tucking under the raw edges. Unfold on one side, then stitch along the inner edge with a ¼-inch (6 mm) seam (figure 3). Fold the strip back over the edge and hand stitch the other side to the triangle.

6. Pin the hood to one corner of the terry cloth square.

7. Trim to round all corners.

8. Machine baste the hood onto the square.

9. Press the six joined strips of print fabric in half lengthwise.

10. Follow the instructions in step 5 and figures 2 and 3 to stitch the binding onto the 34-inch (86.3 cm) square, tucking the strip under where the ends meet.

11. Fold and press the leftover binding into two 5-inch (12.7 cm) long bias strips. Stitch each strip together down the center, making sure to catch the raw edges. Fold each strip into a wing shape and tuck behind the bee appliques.

12. Place bees on outside corner of the towel and machine stitch in place with invisible thread.

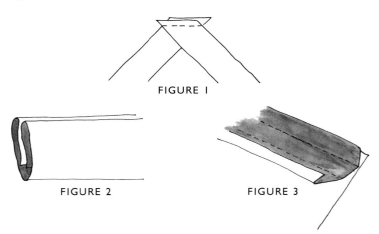

FIGURE I

FIGURE 2

FIGURE 3

WELCOMING BABIES

In rural England, it was traditional to put a crust of bread, a piece of paper containing salt, and a silver coin in a baby's hand before he entered his home. These objects were said to ensure that the baby would never go hungry or thirsty and would be prosperous in the future.

THIS IRRESISTIBLE TOY IS SURE

to become one of Baby's favorites.

The starry arms and legs will give

her many places to grasp and tug,

and the soft texture makes it safe

and inviting to little mouths.

YOU WILL NEED

Template on page 110
½ yard (45.7 cm) of terry cloth
Scissors
Straight pins
Pencil or knitting needle
Felt squares in 3 colors
Embroidery thread
Sewing needle
Sewing machine
Thread
Polyester fiber stuffing
Small bell (optional)

twinkly
STAR TOY

1. Copy the template on page 110.

2. Fold the terry cloth in half, right sides facing. Pin the template to the folded cloth. Add a ⅜-inch (9.5 mm) seam allowance and cut out the template.

3. Machine stitch the star pieces together. Leave the portion that's marked on the template unsewn. Clip the seams as needed. Use a pencil or knitting needle to turn the star right side out.

4. Cut two small circles of felt for the cheeks. Sew them to the large top "face" portion of one side of the star with large running stitches (see page 15).

5. Use embroidery thread to stitch the mouth and hair with a closely spaced running stitch or other straight embroidery stitch. Create the eyes with French knots (see page 14) using six strands of embroidery thread.

6. Stuff the star with polyester fiber stuffing. Add a bell to the stuffing if desired. Hand sew the opening closed.

7. Cut out two felt shapes for the hat—they should be larger than the top point of the star. Hand sew the shapes together along two sides with large running stitches. Cut out a heart or other decorative shape from felt and stitch it to the hat. Slip the hat onto the point. Secure it to the point along the bottom edge with running stitches on both sides.

8. Using very small running stitches, define the facial area by hand sewing both sides of the star together.

just ducky
TOY TOTE AND FLOOR PAD
DESIGNER: JOAN MORRIS

THIS SOFT, WASHABLE PAD *does double duty. On the surface, it's a handy, collapsible toy tote for carrying Baby's many playthings on the road. But pull apart the sides, and it folds out into a cozy floor mat where Baby can play in safety and comfort. This easy-to-make tote is perfect for travel.*

YOU WILL NEED
1 yard (91.4 cm) of patterned flannel fabric
1 yard (91.4 cm) of faux fur fabric
1 yard (91.4 cm) of quilt batting
Scissors
Sewing machine
10 feet (3 m) of web strapping
Thread in coordinating color
1 yard (91.4 cm) of hook-
 and-loop fastener tape
Iron

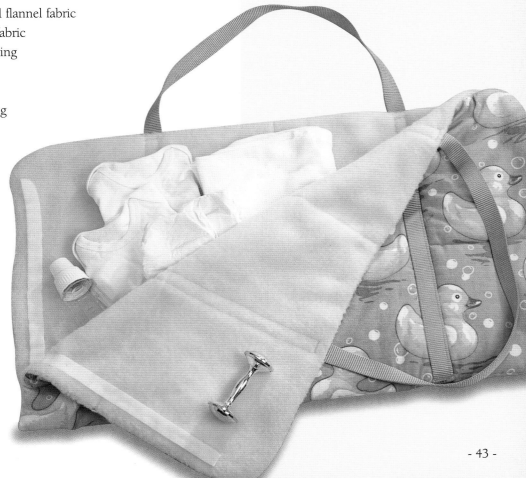

1. Cut the flannel, faux fur, and batting into 30 x 34-inch (76.2 x 86.3 cm) pieces.

2. Place the batting on wrong side of the flannel. Machine baste in place around the edges with a ¼-inch (6 mm) seam allowance.

3. Line up the right side of the faux fur piece with the right side of the flannel and batting piece. Cut around all four corners to make rounded edges.

4. Machine stitch the two pieces together with a ½-inch (1.3 cm) seam allowance. Sew all the way around the edges, leaving an 8-inch (20.3 cm) opening. Clip the curves and turn right side out. Iron. Hand stitch closed.

5. From long edge to long edge, machine stitch three rows, dividing the square into quarters.

6. At the middle stitch, fold the square in half (the middle seam is the bottom of the tote). Measure and mark 7 inches (17.8 cm) in from each edge—this is where you'll position the straps.

7. You'll create the handles with one continuous piece of strapping. Starting at the fold, 7 inches (17.8 cm) in from one side, sew a piece of strapping onto the flannel, sewing up toward the opening of the tote. You'll need to stitch both sides of the strap, close to the edge on each side. Stitch several times to strengthen. When you get to the top of the tote, you'll leave 24 inches (61 cm) of strap loose for a handle, then begin sewing the strap onto the opposite edge of the same side of the tote, 7 inches (17.8 cm) in. Continue sewing to the fold of the tote and beyond, up the other side of the tote. Repeat the process for making the handle as you did on the first side of the tote. Continue sewing the strap onto the tote until you meet the fold where you started.

8. On faux fur side of the tote, stitch hook-and-loop fastener tape to the edges, about ⅛-inch (3 mm) in from the edge.

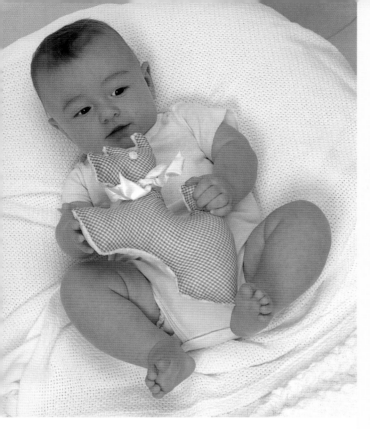

baby's best friend
STUFFED SCOTTIE DOG
DESIGNER: JOAN MORRIS

A GREAT GIFT *for a girl or boy, this stuffed Scottie dog is sure to be at Baby's side for years. Using the template provided, it's easy to make and can even be sewn by hand. As an alternative, stuff the dog with lavender or another fragrant herb and make a drawer sachet.*

YOU WILL NEED
Scottie dog template on page 111
Scissors
¼-yard (22.8 cm) gingham fabric
¼-yard (22.8 cm) upholstery fabric remnant
Straight pins
Sewing machine
1 yard (91.4 cm) of ribbon, ¾ inch (1.9 cm) wide
White thread
Needle
Polyester fiber stuffing
Pencil or knitting needle
White button for eye

1. Copy the Scottie dog template on page 111, enlarging it to the desired size, and cut it out.

2. Place gingham fabric and the upholstery fabric right sides together, pin the template on top of the fabrics, and cut out.

3. Pin the two cut fabric shapes right sides together. Machine stitch together with a ¼-inch (6 mm) seam allowance all the way around the dog, leaving 1 ½ inches (3.8 cm) open near the rear foot.

4. Clip the curves and trim the corners.

5. Turn the dog right side out and push out all the edges using a pencil or knitting needle.

6. Starting at the head, use a pencil or knitting needle to tightly pack pieces of fiber stuffing into the dog.

7. Keep stuffing, working your way back from the head to the back leg opening.

8. Fold in the fabric at the bottom of the leg and hand stitch closed.

9. Double your thread and stitch on the button eye. Be sure it's well attached.

10. Tie a bow with the ribbon at the dog's neck and hand stitch in place.

AS BABY GROWS, IT WILL TAKE *more creativity to keep him occupied. An activity book with removable felt shapes (which you store in a built-in pocket) allows a child to use his imagination and create stories and scenes. You don't need a sewing machine to make it (it's held together with a simple blanket stitch and plenty of craft glue. Since smaller pieces are involved, parents should wait till Baby is at least 18 months old before using this gift.*

four-seasons
FELT ACTIVITY BOOK
DESIGNER: ALLISON SMITH

YOU WILL NEED
Scissors or rotary tool
1 yard (91.4 m) of craft felt in a neutral color
Measuring tape or ruler
Iron
Craft felt squares in a variety of colors
Decorative-edge scissors with loose wavy pattern (optional)
Iron-on fusible webbing
Craft glue
Paintbrush
Embroidery thread
Large-eye needle
Puff fabric paint

1. Cut three pieces of the neutral color felt into rectangles, each 8 x 16 inches (20.3 x 40.6 cm). Fold each rectangle in half, and press flat. Each half of the rectangle will be a page in the book.

2. Cut three pieces of felt in the same color into 5-inch (12.7 cm) squares.

3. Cut "landscape" pieces from squares of craft felt. For the page shown, we used green for grass. The landscape pieces should be as long as the width of each page and take up no more than one-third of the page when aligned with the bottom. You can use decorative-edge scissors to make the variations in the landscape represent grass, snow, sand, etc.

4. Attach the fusible webbing to the back of each landscape piece following the manufacturer's instructions. Peel off the paper backing.

```
┌─────────────────────┬─────────────────────┐
│                     │                     │
│    ┌──────────┐     │                     │
│    │          │     │                     │
│    │ B        │     │                     │
│    │          │     │   ∿∿∿∿∿∿∿∿∿∿∿      │
│    └──────────┘     │         A           │
│                     │                     │
└─────────────────────┴─────────────────────┘
```

FIGURE I

5. Open one of the large rectangles you folded in step 1, and press a landscape piece (A) in place on the right side of the fold, aligned with the bottom (see figure 1). Press to activate the glue. Repeat for each of the rectangles and landscape pieces.

6. On the left side of the fold in each rectangle, center one of the 5-inch (12.7 cm) squares (B) you cut in step 2 (figure 1). Glue the bottom and two sides of the square to the page with the craft glue, leaving the top edge unglued to form a pocket.

7. Fold the pages closed again, and press the fold. Stack the three rectangles on top of one another. Use a large-eye needle and embroidery thread to stitch them together with a blanket stitch (see page 14).

8. Cut out small shapes and figures from the remaining felt squares. Paint details on the figures with the fabric paint.

In many cultures around the world, babies are first given a false name before a real name. The false name is meant to confuse and trick evil spirits which may try to harm or steal the newborn. After a baby has sucessfully made it through the inital months of life, a real name is usually bestowed on him at a naming ceremony.

dots and flowers
DECOUPAGE SHELF
DESIGNER: ALLISON SMITH

YOU WILL NEED
Unfinished wooden peg shelf
Spray primer
White spray paint
Printed tissue paper
Scissors
Decoupage medium
Foam brush
Craft paint in coordinating color
½-inch (1.3 cm) paintbrush
Flower sponge stamp
Artist's brush (optional)

1. Prime the shelf with the spray primer. Allow to dry.

2. Paint the shelf with two coats of white spray paint. Allow to dry.

3. Cut a piece of tissue paper that is slightly larger than the top of the shelf. Paint the top of the shelf with a thin coat of decoupage medium. If it's too thick, dilute it with a little water.

4. Carefully place the tissue paper on top of the shelf. Smooth it down as much as possible, but be gentle—the tissue tears easily. Paint over the tissue with a second coat of decoupage medium to seal it.

5. Apply paint to the stamp with a small paintbrush. Stamp flowers across the front of the shelf. With a small brush, fill in any spots that didn't absorb the paint.

BABIES COME INTO THE WORLD
with nothing but their irresistible personalities, but they're soon surrounded by a lot of stuff. Lotions and powders, burp cloths and diapers (not to mention all the toys) quickly accumulate in the nursery. What most parents need is more storage space. Premade peg shelves do the trick, and easy to dress up with printed tissue paper decoupage and sponge stamps.

good little eater
OILCLOTH BIB
DESIGNER: JOAN MORRIS

ON THE HIGHCHAIR, *on the floor—baby food ends up everywhere except in Baby's mouth. That's where bibs come in. These bibs are easy to make from oilcloth, a classic material for tablecloths, and the perfect solution for messy little eaters. It wipes clean, saving Mom and Dad valuable time. Try making the bib in vinyl too, and backing it with a hand towel. Both styles are charming, practical, and make great gifts.*

YOU WILL NEED
Templates on page 112
Scissors
2 pieces of oilcloth in contrasting patterns for the bib and pocket, ¼ yard (22.86 cm) each
Straight pins
½-inch (1.2 cm) wide double-fold bias tape
1 x 1-inch (2.5 x 2.5 cm) piece of hook-and-loop fastener tape
Sewing machine
Coordinating thread

1. Copy the bib template on page 112, enlarging it to the size you want for your bib. Cut out the copy, pin it to the oilcloth, and cut the oilcloth. Copy the pocket template, enlarging it until it fits across the bottom of the bib. Repeat the same process for marking, pinning, and cutting the pocket fabric.

2. Cut a piece of bias tape to fit the length of the top of the pocket piece. Fold the tape over the top of the pocket and machine stitch it in place.

3. Align the bottom of the pocket with the bottom of the bib and machine baste in place.

In an old German custom, a baby was taken on her first outing at about six or seven weeks of age. Well-wishers would tap the baby's lips three times with a *Schwatzei,* or "talking egg," to ensure that she would learn to speak quickly.

4. Fold a length of bias tape over the edges of the whole bib and machine stitch in place, easing the tape as you go.

5. Attach a 1-inch (2.5 cm) square of hook-and-loop fastener tape to each side of the neck closure, one on the patterned side and one on the back side of the material.

VARIATION

If you can't find oilcloth, you can use vinyl or even a vinyl tablecloth backed with a hand towel. It's machine washable, and you can even machine dry it on low heat.

YOU WILL NEED
Bib template on page 112
Scissors
Straight pins
¼ yard (22.86 cm) of patterned vinyl
Hand towel in coordinating color
Thread in coordinating color
Sewing machine
½-inch (1.2 cm) double-fold bias tape
Hook-and-loop fastener tape

1. Copy the bib template on page 112, and follow the process described in step 1 on page 51 to cut the fabric.

2. Pin the bib shape, wrong-side down, in the center of the hand towel.

3. Machine baste the bib and hand towel together.

4. Cut the hand towel to match the bib shape.

5. Machine stitch ½-inch (1.2 cm) bias tape all the way around the edge of the bib, easing the tape as you go.

6. Attach the hook-and-loop fastener tape to the neck closure as described in step 5 on page 51.

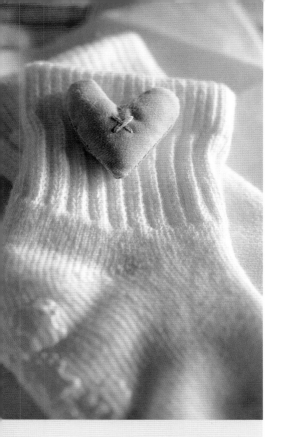

WELCOMING BABIES

In Korea, the biggest celebration for a new baby is held 100 days after his birth. The *pak il,* as the party is called, is a big feast that marks the baby's survival of the first critical period of life. Traditional gifts given at this time are silver chopsticks, clothing, or a gold ring. The ring was seen as a sort of insurance policy against hard times in the future. It could always be sold or melted down in times of need.

sweet
LITTLE SOCKS

MOST BABIES SPEND *their first year in stocking feet, so parents need plenty of socks. Give plain white socks a little more interest with a simple embellishment that takes just minutes to complete. These sweet little socks look adorable and won't get lost in the laundry!*

YOU WILL NEED
Heart template on page 120
Purchased socks
Scissors
Cotton fabric
Coordinating thread
Embroidery thread
Large-eye needle
Cotton batting or polyester fiber stuffing
Pencil

1. Copy the heart template on page 120, enlarging or reducing it to fit the socks.

2. Lay the template on the cotton fabric. You don't need to pin it or be exact—just cut around the shape. Repeat for a second heart, and then cut a second pair of hearts for the second sock.

3. Lay two cutout hearts right sides together, and hand stitch them together with a ¼-inch (6 mm) seam allowance, leaving about ½ inch (1.3 cm) open.

4. Stick a pencil through the opening and turn the fabric right side out.

5. Use the pencil to push batting or fiber stuffing through the opening, then hand stitch it closed.

6. Center your heart on the side of the sock. Pull a threaded needle through the sock and heart starting from the inside, then back out to form a cross stitch. Knot the thread on the inside.

A SCENTED SACHET BAG

is a sweet gift for a nursery. It looks charming hanging on a door or drawer handle, and fills the room with the soothing smell of lavender. To make this sachet pouch, find a beautifully decorated antique linen tea towel at a flea market or an antique store. You'll need silk ribbon, stuffing, dried lavender, and simple machine stitching to hold it all together.

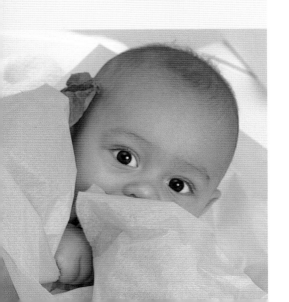

vintage tea-towel
LAVENDER SACHET BAG
DESIGNER: ALLISON SMITH

YOU WILL NEED
Vintage tea towel with lace embellishment
Measuring tape
Scissors
Coordinating thread
Sewing machine
2 yards (1.82 m) of silk ribbon
Fray retardant
½-yard (45.7 cm) of lightweight cotton or organdy fabric
   in coordinating color
Polyester fiber stuffing
Dried lavender or other herb

1. Trim the long edges of the towel so that it's 7 inches (7.8 cm) wide.

2. Measure 11 inches (27.9 cm) up from the lacy edge and cut. Fold the cut short edge under and hem using a very small stitch.

3. From the remaining piece of the tea towel, cut a 5 x 7-inch (12.7 x 17.8 cm) square.

4. Fold the ribbon in half. Pin the center of the ribbon to the center of one side of the square you made in step 3, attaching the two pieces at the edges. Easing the ribbon as you go, start sewing the ribbon to the square, working out to both sides. Keep in mind that the raw edges need to be facing in.

5. Find the back center of the undecorated end of the tea towel—this will be on the "wrong" side of the towel, i.e., the opposite end and opposite side from the decoration. Pin the center of the other long edge of the ribbon in place, just as you did in step 4. Sew the ribbon as you did in step 4, raw edges facing in, working out from the bottom center up the sides. Stop sewing when you reach the point parallel to the top of the square. The lacy end of the tea towel will now be a flap, and you will have created a pocket.

6. Snip the corners and spray the fabric with fray retardant.

7. Turn the pocket right side out and press.

8. Trim the ends of the ribbon and treat them with fray check.

9. Cut two pieces of the coordinating fabric to the dimensions of the square you created in step 3.

10. Sew the two squares together with right sides together, leaving a 2-inch (5.2 cm) opening.

11. Turn right-side out and press.

12. Fill with polyester fiber stuffing and lavender. Stitch the opening closed.

13. Insert the sachet into the pocket.

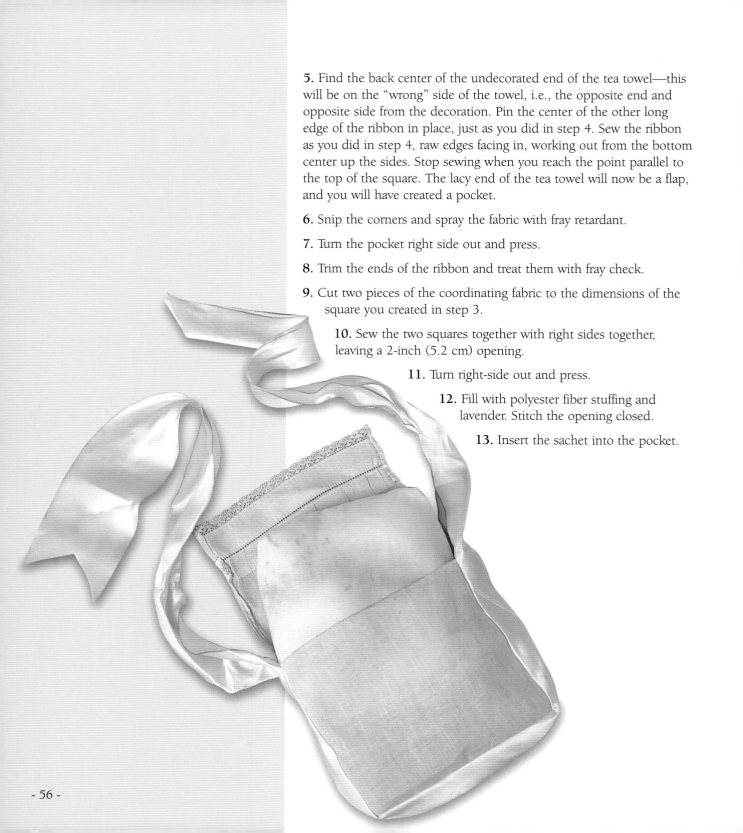

WHEN BABIES LEARN TO GRASP,

a rattle is usually one of the first things they reach for. It's great to see a baby's face when he discovers that he can hold something in his hand, shake it, and make a noise, all by himself. This rattle is bright, soft, and safe, so when it ends up in Baby's mouth (as it inevitably will), parents don't need to worry. It's also very simple to make. You can hand sew it together in minutes—just make sure you use strong thread so it will stand up to frequent use.

color-slice
FELT RATTLE

YOU WILL NEED
Template on page 113
Felt squares in eight different colors
Scissors
Straight pins
Sewing needle
Strong thread or embroidery floss
Bell or other noisemaker
Pencil or knitting needle
Polyester or cotton fiber stuffing

1. Photocopy the template on page 113, enlarging it to desired size.

2. Pin the template to your first piece of felt and cut around it. Repeat for each of the remaining seven colors of felt.

3. Thread the needle with a doubled length of thread. Hand sew one side of two felt pieces together with a simple running stitch (see page 15). The seam should not be much wider than ⅛ inch (3 mm). Knot the thread at the end of each row of stitching.

4. Continue to add a felt piece to the previously joined pieces. When you sew the very last piece joining the rattle, leave a couple of inches unsewn.

5. Stuff the rattle with fiber stuffing, using a pencil or a knitting needle to pack it tightly. Add one or more bells to the stuffing well inside the rattle.

6. Hand sew the opening closed.

ALTHOUGH BABIES CAN'T GRAB

things or even sit up for months, a mobile can capture their attention almost from birth. The swirling shapes and colors can keep them fascinated for hours and help to develop their sense of sight. This mobile is easy to make with purchased stuffed animals. When Baby gets bigger, the mobile can be disassembled so the animals can be used as toys.

flying friends
MOBILE

YOU WILL NEED
2 yards (1.8 m) of colored cording
Scissors
Measuring tape or ruler
Wooden bead with wide hole opening
Large wooden hoop or ring
Pencil or marker
Sewing needle
Coordinating thread
4 to 5 small purchased stuffed animals
Acrylic paint (optional)
*Safety note: Once a baby gets big enough to reach and grab for things (about five months) the mobile should be removed from the crib.

1. Cut a length of cord for each stuffed animal. The length of your cord will vary, depending on the height of the ceiling and the height of the crib. Count on needing a length of at least 4 feet (1.2 m) from the ceiling to the wooden bead. Allow about 8 inches (20.3 cm) between the wooden bead and the ring, and about 1 inch (2.5 cm) from the ring to the top of each animal's head.

2. Knot the pieces of cord together on one end, about 4 inches (10.2 cm) from the end. Twist the cords together to about 1 foot (30.4 cm) from the bottom, and then thread the twisted cord through the wooden bead, and knot.

3. You'll have about 1 foot (30.4 cm) of loose cord under the knot. Choose equidistant spots on your wooden hoop, and mark. Starting with one piece of cord, wrap the cord around the hoop and knot, leaving about 2 inches (5.2 cm) of loose cord at the end. Repeat for each remaining piece of cord.

4. Securely stitch one end of each piece of cord to the top of each animal's head with a needle and thread.

5. Wrap the leftover cord around the wooden hoop, and tuck in the ends.

6. If desired, paint your wooden bead to complement the cord color and the stuffed animals.

will quickly become the favorite
accessory of a new mom. It fits
around her waist to make nursing or
bottle feeding more comfortable. You
can customize it for Mom's size,
making the opening wider than the
ones you find in stores. When Baby
gets a little bigger, but can't quite
sit up, parents can prop her in the
middle of the pillow for playtime.

nursing
AND PLAY PILLOW

DESIGNER: ALLISON SMITH

YOU WILL NEED

Template on page 114
Scissors
Cotton print fabric, about 1 yard (91.4 cm)
Straight pins
Sewing machine
Iron
Polyester fiber stuffing
Sewing needle
Thread

1. Copy the template on page 114, enlarging it to the size you need, and modifying the opening size, if necessary, to fit the mom you're making it for. Cut out the pattern.

2. Fold the fabric in half. Place the pattern on the fabric, lining it up on the folded edge.

3. Pin the pattern down and cut out the fabric. DO NOT cut along the folded edge! Remove the pattern and unfold the fabric.

4. Layer the two pieces of fabric with right sides together, and machine stitch, leaving a 4-inch (10.2 cm) opening.

5. Trim the seams. Snip the seams at the curves. Turn the fabric right-side out and press.

6. Stuff with polyester fiber stuffing, and whipstitch (see page 15) the opening closed.

IT'S HARD TO KEEP UP WITH
the clutter of a growing collection of
toys, but this ingenious toy basket is
a smart solution. It rolls on a platform, so toys can be thrown in the
top and pushed out of the way or
moved easily to another room. Once
Baby becomes a toddler and can pull
the platform, the rolling basket itself
becomes a toy, making clean up time
fun. The basket liner is removable
and has a drawstring, making it
useful for travel.

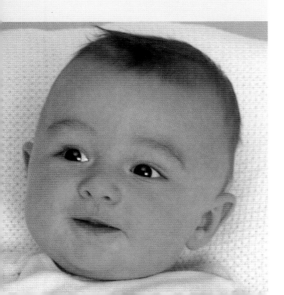

good times
ROLLING TOY BASKET
DESIGNER: MIEGAN GORDON

YOU WILL NEED
8 x 72-inch (20.3 cm x 1.8 m) board

Measuring tape

Level (optional)

Table saw

Jigsaw

Power drill with #6 and #8 countersink bits

Polyurethane finish

16 flat-head sheet metal screws, #6 x 1 ¼ inches (3.2 cm)

4 flat-head sheet metal screws, #8 x 1 ½ inches (3.8 cm)

Toy block or piece of scrap wood for handle, approximately
    ¾ x ¾ x 4 inches (1.9 x 1.9 x 10.2 cm)

4 swivel casters, each 1 1/2 inches (3.8 cm) in diameter*

Small screws for attaching swivel casters

Screwdriver

Purchased laundry basket, approximately 12 inches (30.5 cm) high,
    19 inches (48.3 cm) in diameter

Spray paint (optional)

6 ½-foot (1.9 m) length of nylon rope

1 to 2 yards (91.22 cm to 1.82 m) of heavy cotton fabric,
    printed on both sides

Scissors

Coordinating thread

Sewing machine

Safety pin

*If you like, buy two locking and two nonlocking casters. Mount the locking casters
on the back of the platform to act as brakes so that Baby can't pull the basket before
he's ready.

1. Cut your wood with a table saw according to the diagram (see figure 1).

2. Determine the right side of the 2-foot (61 cm) pieces and round two corners of each piece with the jigsaw.

3. You'll need one hole for the pull rope on each of the 2 foot (61 cm) rounded edge pieces. Determine the location of the holes—they'll each be ½-inch (1.3 cm) in diameter—and drill.

4. Align the toy block or piece of scrap wood over the holes you drilled in step 3 and drill corresponding holes in it. If you like, paint the handle. Sand all the pieces and apply a polyurethane finish. Let dry.

5. With the right sides down, align the 2-foot (61 cm) pieces side by side (rounded corners facing out). Now you'll connect the two pieces with two crosspieces. Cut your 1-foot (30.5 cm) long crosspiece in half width-wise. You'll have two 4-inch (10.2 cm) pieces. Position the 1-foot (30.5 cm) crosspieces width-wise at either end of the platform, about 6 inches (15.2 cm) from the edge.

6. Attach the crosspieces to the 2-foot (61 cm) pieces by predrilling eight holes in each crosspiece with the #6 countersink bits. Position your holes on each edge of the crosspiece, approximately 3 inch (7.6 cm) apart.

7. Attach the swivel casters to each end of the underside of the platform according to the manufacturer's instructions. The casters should be about 1 inch (2.5 cm) in from the edges.

8. If you like, spray paint the basket before attaching it to the platform. Use the remaining 1-foot (30.5 cm) scrap to cut two pieces to fit into the bottom of the basket—they don't have to be cut to the same size since they won't show. Predrill two equidistant holes in each scrap piece with the #8 countersink bit. Position the basket on the platform, and then screw through the scrap and basket into the platform to attach it.

9. Knot one end of the rope, and then thread the loose end up through one of the holes you drilled in the platform in step 3. Pull the rope through one of the holes in the handle, and then through the other. Decide how long you want the rope pull to be, cut or adjust as necessary, and then thread it back through the other hole in the platform and knot.

FIGURE I

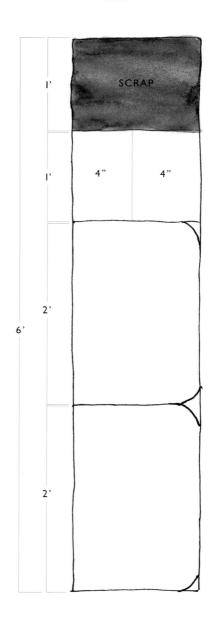

TO MAKE THE BASKET LINER

10. To determine the size of the basket liner, calculate the circumference of the basket, divide that figure in half, and add 2 inches (5.2 cm). Write down the measurement. Measure the depth of the basket and add 4 inches (10.2 cm) to that figure for the lip that hangs over the edge of the basket. Cut two rectangles of fabric to your measurements.

11. Cut a circle 2 inches (5.2 cm) larger than the inside bottom of the basket.

12. Cut a bias strip 2 inches (5.2 cm) wide and the same length as the circumference of the circle you cut in step 11.

13. Machine sew the two rectangles together along the short sides with French seams (see figure 2). Sew the wrong sides of the rectangles together using a ¼ inch (6 mm) seam allowance. Trim the fabric close to the seam. Turn wrong side out (right sides together) and stitch again catching the loose inside edges and securing them. These will be the sides of the basket liner.

FIGURE 2

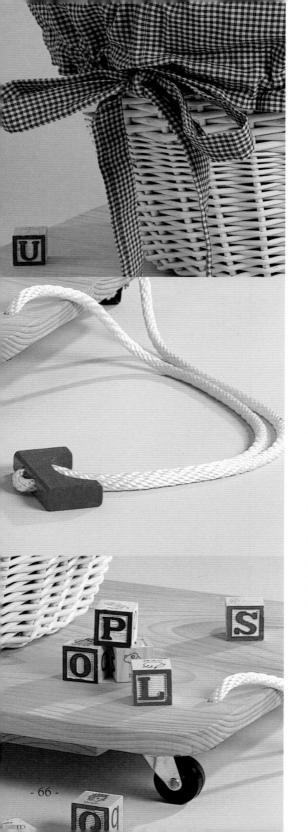

14. Sew the bottom circle to the sides, pleating or gathering as necessary. Cover the seam allowance with the bias strip and sew the strip in place.

15. Turn over a seam allowance on the top of the liner and press.

16. You'll be making a separate strip for the drawstring casing. Measure the circumference of the top of the liner, decide what width you'd like the casing to be, and then cut the casing strip. Turn under a seam allowance on one long edge of the casing and press. Next, turn under a seam allowance on a short edge of the casing, press, and machine stitch in place.

17. Pin the casing to the top of the liner. You'll need an opening of about 1 ½ inches (3.8 cm) where the ends of the casing won't meet so that you can get your drawstring through and tie it in a bow.

18. Topstitch the casing to the liner, stitching about ⅛ inch (3 mm) from the bottom, and meeting the turned-over seam allowance of the liner on the top edge.

19. To make the drawstring, add 2 feet (61 cm) to the circumference of the top of the liner, and cut a 3-inch wide (7.6 cm) strip to that measurement (you may need to join two pieces of fabric to get that length).

20. Fold the strip, right sides together, and stitch along the long edge with a ¼-inch (6 mm) seam allowance. Stitch across one short end. Use a pencil to turn the fabric inside out and stitch the second end closed. Use a safety pin to pull the drawstring through the casing.

elfin
SLIPPERS

YOU WILL NEED
Pair of booties or slipper socks
Skein of yarn, at least 7 yards (6.4 m)
2 x 3-inch (5.2 x 7.6 cm) piece of cardboard
Scissors
Large-eye tapestry needle

1. Wind off a 6-yard (5.4 m) length of yarn. Cut it off. Cut off an additional 4-inch (10.2 cm) length of yarn.

2. Wrap the long length of yarn around the 3-inch (7.6 cm) side of the cardboard. Pack the yarn tightly, winding back over the yarn you've already wrapped if necessary. Loosely tie the short length of yarn around the wrapped yarn. Do not tie it tightly.

3. Bend the cardboard slightly, and slip the wound yarn off the cardboard. Keep the yarn gathered together. Tighten the short length of yarn to gather the pompom in the center. Tie it tightly.

4. Cut the doubled ends of the pompom. Fluff the pompom, trimming as needed.

5. Thread one end of the 4-inch (10.2 cm) length of yarn in the needle. Bring the needle through the bootie. Re-thread the needle with the second length and bring it through the bootie. Tie the ends securely and trim.

6. Create a second pompom and attach it to the bootie.

BABY FEET ARE SO CUTE

that it's a shame to cover them up. Adding a pompom to purchased slippers or booties creates a look that's so adorable, it's the next best thing to bare baby feet. It's so easy to do that you'll be able to make several pairs with different colors of yarn. Once you've gotten the hang of it, try adding pompoms to a purchased hat or mittens, too.

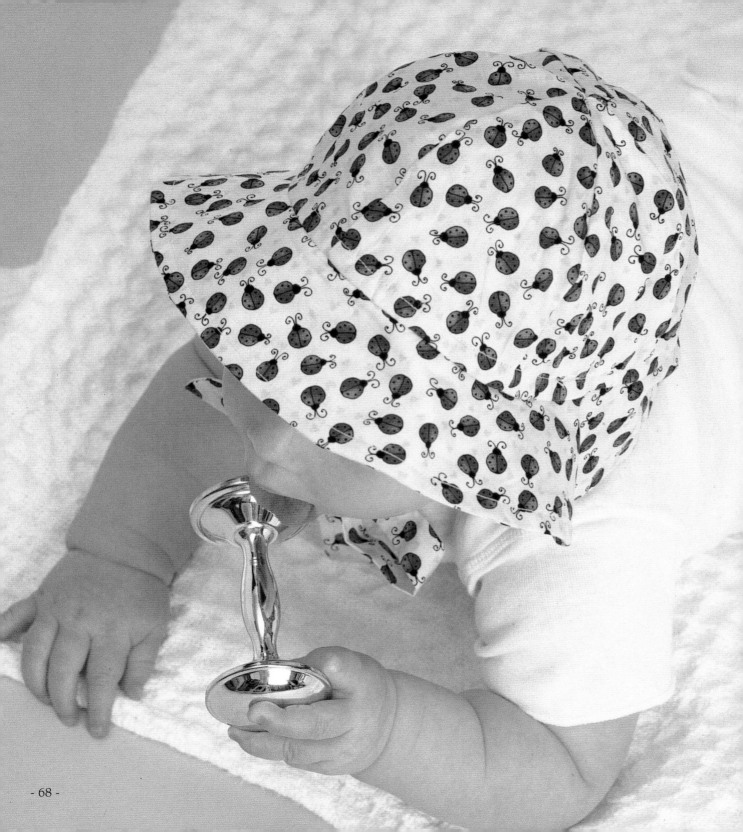

A BABY'S DELICATE SKIN

needs protection from the strong summer sun, and this floppy-brimmed sunhat is the perfect solution. The construction is simple and foolproof. If you have a sewing machine, you can make it in a few hours. A perfect gift, this is the hat parents will reach for again and again in the summer.

little ladybug
SUNHAT
DESIGNER: JOAN MORRIS

YOU WILL NEED
Templates on page 115
1 yard (91.4 cm) of print fabric
Straight pins (optional)
Fabric marker or pencil
Scissors
Sewing machine
Thread in coordinating color
½ yard (45.7 cm) of fusible webbing
Iron

1. Copy the templates on page 115, enlarging them to the size you want. Use the templates as patterns to mark and cut 12 hat top pieces, two hat brim pieces, and two hat tie pieces each 2 x 18 inches (5.1 x 45.7 cm).

2. Machine stitch the right sides of three top pieces together with a ¼-inch (6 mm) seam, starting from the point, moving down to the wide bottom side. Repeat with the three remaining top pieces.

3. Stitch the two three-panel top pieces together.

4. Repeat steps 2 and 3 for the remaining six top pieces to create the hat facing (inside top).

5. With wrong sides together, pin the hat top to the hat facing, matching the seams. Baste the raw edges together at the wide bottom.

6. Use the brim template to cut a brim piece from the fusible webbing, and apply it (following manufacturer's instructions) to the wrong side of one hat brim piece to reinforce it.

7. Turn the two brim pieces right sides together and machine stitch at the center seam with a ½-inch (1.3 cm) seam allowance.

8. Trim the seams and clip the curves. Turn the brim right side out and press. Baste the raw edges together.

9. On the outside edge of the brim, machine topstitch (see page 15) ¼ inch (6 mm) in from the outer edge.

10. Pin the brim to the outside of the top of the hat. Machine stitch the two parts together with a ½-inch (1.3 cm) seam allowance.

12. Fold each 2 x 18-inch (5.1 x 45.7 cm) tie piece in half lengthwise, right sides together. Stitch the long sides using a ¼-inch (6 mm) seam allowance. Stitch one short end closed and leave the other open. Repeat for other tie piece.

13. With a pencil or knitting needle, turn both

14. Find the back seam of the brim. Measure around in each direction to find the center where you'll place the ties. Put the raw edge of the first tie inside the hat, matching it to the raw edge of the brim. Stitch the tie in place (see photo above). Repeat for the other tie.

15. Press the raw edges of the brim up into the hat. Stitch ¼ inch (6 mm) up from the seam all the way around, catching the raw edges and ties.

WELCOMING BABIES

Traditionally, Chinese parents have waited until their baby is one month old to give him or her a name. The name was announced at a ceremony called a Red Egg and Ginger Party. Eggs are a symbol of fertility everywhere, but in China, white is the color associated with mourning, so eggs (usually duck eggs), were hard-boiled and dyed red, the color of good fortune. The eggs were sent to friends and relatives as an invitation to the baby-naming ceremony. Those who received an egg came to the parents' home with gifts of "lucky money" enclosed in red envelopes called *li-shi.* A baby girl would often receive jewelry that would be put away and used as part of her dowry.

THE FLOWERS ON THIS

lampshade come from a surprising source—they're simply transferred from paper party napkins! Choose napkins with motifs that match the nursery décor, or if you don't know it, choose neutral-colored soft designs. Cut the designs off the napkins and decoupage them onto a purchased shade. It's a simple way to create a soothing glow in Baby's first room.

sweetheart
SHADE
DESIGNER: TERRY TAYLOR

YOU WILL NEED
Sharp scissors
Decorative napkins
Pencil
Plain lampshade (paper shades work best)
Decoupage medium
Small paintbrush
Stencil brush

1. Use sharp scissors to cut out the design elements you wish to use from the napkins. Set them aside. The decorative napkins have two or more layers—you probably discovered this while you were cutting out the design elements. Peel the printed layer away from the under layer.

2. Arrange the cutout design elements on the shade. When you're pleased with the way they look, draw light pencil marks on the shade around the elements to guide you when you glue them down. This is especially important if your pattern is a repeating pattern, not so important if it's an unstructured arrangement.

3. Using a paintbrush, spread a thin coat of decoupage medium on the shade in approximately the same size as one of the cutout shapes

4. Place the pattern element on the shade. Use a stencil brush and a straight up-and-down pouncing motion to adhere the element to the shade. You may need to add a bit of medium around the edges of the pattern. Use a small brush to paint medium under the edges. Repeat the process until you're pleased with the design. Allow the shade to dry overnight.

THE WINTER BABY NEEDS

THE WINTER BABY NEEDS

a hat when she's outdoors, and

this elfin one is warm, cozy, and

irresistibly cute. It's very simple to

make with fleecy fabric, and metallic

thread gives it a magical feel. The

little bell rings when Baby's head

moves, adding a delightful sound that

will bring a smile to parents' faces.

YOU WILL NEED

½ yard (45.7 cm) of fleece fabric

Scissors

Thread in coordinating color

Sewing machine

Sewing needle

Small square of felt

Heart templates on page 110

Scrap or small piece of organdy

Gold metallic thread

Small sequins

Small bell

Gold embroidery thread

Pencil

*Measure the circumference of the baby's head for the hat size. It should be at least 15 to 16 inches (38.1 to 40.6 cm).

baby
PIXIE HAT
DESIGNER: EMMA PEARSON

1. Cut the fleece fabric into two pieces according to the diagram (see figure 1).

2. Machine stitch sides A and B of the triangle together with a ¼-inch (6 mm) seam allowance.

3. Machine stitch the two sides of the rectangle together.

FIGURE I

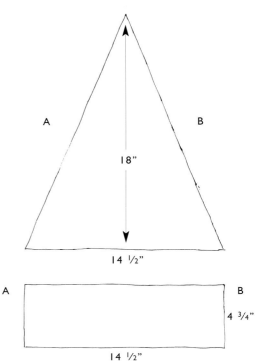

4. Machine stitch the band you created in step 3 to side C of the triangle, with a ¼-inch (6 mm) seam allowance. Make sure the seams meet.

5. Tuck under the bottom of the band to form a hem. Machine stitch the hem with gold metallic thread using a zigzag stitch.

6. Sew the sequins on randomly on the bottom of the band with the metallic thread (use a zigzag stitch).

7. Copy the heart templates on page 110. Cut three small hearts out of colored felt, using the template as a guide. Cut three smaller hearts out of the organdy, and use gold embroidery thread to sew the smaller hearts on top of the larger felt ones.

8. Find the center front of the hat and hand sew the largest center heart on using gold embroidery thread. Position and sew the other two hearts in relation to the first.

9. Use gold embroidery thread to sew stars (see figure 2) in a random pattern on the pointed area of the hat.

10. Securely sew the bell to the tip of the hat's point using gold embroidery thread.

FIGURE 2

START HERE

NEWBORN BABIES LOVE

to be swaddled, and a snug fleece bunting is the ultimate in warmth and comfort. This cozy bunting has charming details and is easy to make with simple materials. It's a perfect coming-home-from-the-hospital present for a winter baby.

baby
BUNTING
DESIGNER: EMMA PEARSON

YOU WILL NEED

1 ½ yards (1.37 m) of fleece fabric

Scissors

Coordinating thread

Sewing machine

Straight pins

Large-eye needle

3 bundles of silk embroidery thread

Felt squares in 3 different colors*

Silver metallic thread

Polymer clay in color of your choice

Rubber stamp or object of your choice for button design

Oven

Beads for tassel (optional)

*usually sold in 9 x 12-inch (23 x 31 cm) pieces

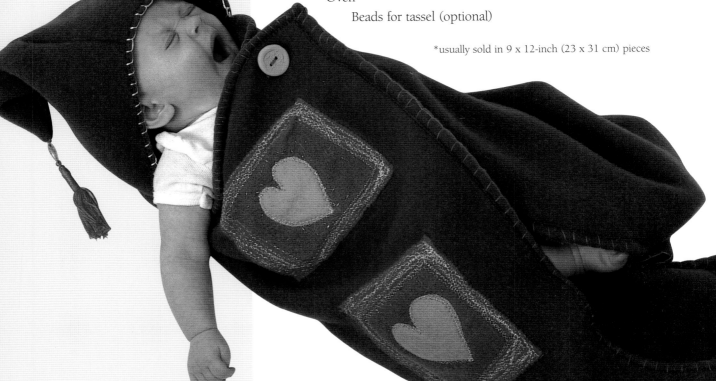

FIGURE 1

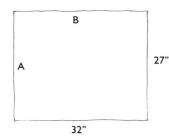

B

A

27"

32"

FIGURE 2

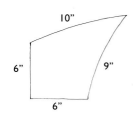

10"

6"

9"

6"

FIGURE 3

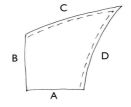

C

B

D

A

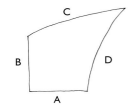

C

B

D

A

FIGURE 4

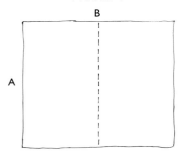

B

A

FIGURE 5

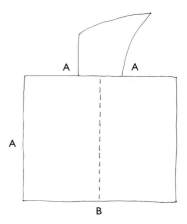

A

A

A

B

1. Cut a 27 x 32-inch (69.9 x 81.2 cm) rectangle from the fleece (see figure 1).

2. Tuck under a ¼-inch (6 mm) hem all around the rectangle, and machine stitch in place.

3. Cut two more pieces of fleece to the dimensions shown in figure 2. These pieces will become the hood.

4. Sew the hood together, side C to C and D to D (see figure 3).

5. Tuck a ¼-inch (6 mm) hem under side B of the hood and machine stitch in place (this will be the hood's opening).

6. Fold the rectangle in half and place a pin at the center fold (see figure 4).

7. Center the back seam of the hood over the pin that you positioned in step 6 (see figure 5). Sew side A of the hood to the rectangle.

8. Blanket stitch (see page 14) all the way around the edge of the rectangle using silk embroidery thread (you'll probably need two bundles).

TO MAKE THE DECORATIVE PANELS

9. Cut two pieces of colored felt in one color, each about 4 x 6 inches (10 x 15.2 cm).

10. Cut another two pieces of felt in another color, each about 3 x 4 inches (8 x 10 cm).

11. Cut two hearts out of a third color of felt, sizing them to fit inside the smaller rectangle.

12. Machine stitch one small rectangle to a larger one using silver thread and a zigzag stitch. Repeat for the additional rectangles.

13. Machine stitch a heart shape to the center of the smaller rectangle using the silver metallic thread and a zigzag stitch. Repeat for the additional heart and rectangle.

14. Fold the bunting as shown in the diagram (see figure 6). Place the felt rectangles on the front of the bunting in whatever position you'd like. Remember to leave room for the buttons on the top edge near the hood. Hand sew the rectangles onto the bunting with the embroidery thread.

TO MAKE THE BUTTONS

15. Form two small circles from polymer clay and flatten until they are about 2 ½ inches (6.35 cm) in diameter.

16. Find a textured design you like, such as a rubber stamp or a piece of jewelry. Press the texture into the clay circle to leave a clear impression (you can always reflatten and start over again if your first pressing doesn't work).

FIGURE 6

17. Use a straight pin to create two neat holes in the circle for the buttonholes. Make sure the holes are not too close to the edge and that the hole is wide enough to accommodate the embroidery thread.

18. Bake the buttons in an oven according to the manufacturer's instructions.

19. The buttons will be on the back side of the rectangle when it's opened out. Fold the left side of the rectangle inward, and cross over the right side. The buttons will be on the underside flap, and the buttonholes will be on the outside flap (see figure 7). Position buttons on the fleece where you want them, approximately 2 inches (5.2 cm) in from the edge and 1 inch (2.5 cm) down.

20. To make the buttonholes, cut a slit to the same diameter as the button. Machine or hand sew an overstitch around the slit to keep it from getting wider.

TO MAKE THE TASSEL ON THE HOOD

21. Cut off about 27 ½ inches (70 cm) from one bundle of embroidery thread. Fold this bundle in half. Unravel about 1 yard (95.4 cm) of embroidery thread, but don't cut it. Wrap this piece around the top of the bundle you folded in the previous step. Save a little extra at the end to form a tight knot and a small loop (see figure 8).

22. Cut the bottom of the tassel to make the threads line up. Add beads for interest if desired, then sew the tassel securely to the tip of the hood.

FIGURE 7

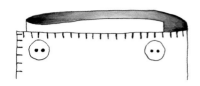

FIGURE 8

I.

2.

3.

4.

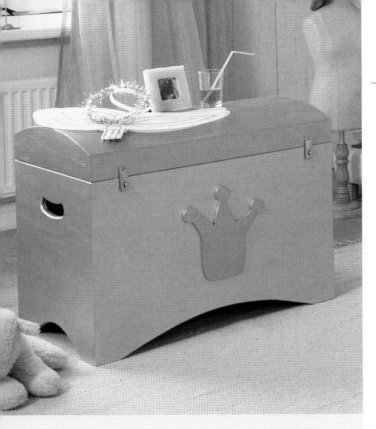

YOU WILL NEED

Crown template on page 118

Unfinished wood toy chest or box with lid

Pencil

¼-inch (6 mm) basswood or interior-grade plywood

Jigsaw*

Fine-grit sandpaper

Wood glue

Small wire brads (optional)

Hammer (optional)

Silver-tone hinges (optional)**

Silver-tone closure hardware (optional)

Silver acrylic paint

*Follow standard safety procedures for working with a saw.

**If you decide to put a hinge on the chest, make sure you use a child-safe hinge that locks in place when open. Toddlers can pull the lid open themselves, so you must be sure that the lid won't close on their fingers once it's opened.

BABY'S SPECIAL TREASURES *deserve a special place in the nursery. It's easy to transform an unfinished wooden box into a treasure chest with a little paint and very simple carpentry. When Baby is bigger, she'll love to store her most precious possessions inside it.*

1. Copy the crown template on page 118. If you like, make copies in several different sizes and decide which size looks best on your toy chest.

2. Trace the template onto the basswood. Cut it out with a jigsaw.

3. Sand the cut edge of the crown.

4. Spread a thin coat of wood glue on the back of the crown. Place it on the toy chest as desired. You may also use a few small wire brads to further secure the crown. Let the glue dry. If the box doesn't already have hardware, you can attach hinges to the back of the box and lid, and closure hardware to the front.

5. Paint the chest with acrylic paints, or simply paint the crown.

baby's first
COUNTING BOOK
DESIGNER: MIEGAN GORDON

A BABY'S FIRST BOOKS *should be simple—bright, eye-catching images and not too much text. This soft handmade counting book is a great example, and a perfect introduction to numbers. Baby will be fascinated by the bright colors and enjoy the soft touch. It's easy to make and machine washable (on the gentle cycle).*

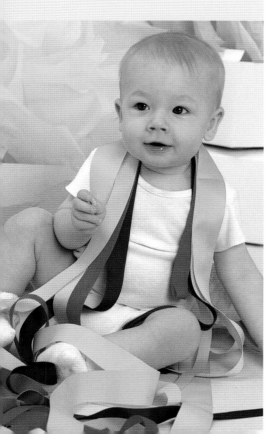

1. Cut the canvas into 11 pieces, each 10 inches x 20 ⅔ (26.7 x 52.7 cm). Fold each piece in half and press. You'll have 11 rectangles, each 10 x 10 ¼ inches (25.4 x 26 cm). These are the book's pages.

2. On each page, topstitch (see page 15) a seam ¼ inch (6 mm) in from the folded edge and ½-inch (1.3 cm) in from the other three edges.

3. You'll need holes for the binding on one edge of each page. Decide where you want the holes to be, and mark the spots with a pencil on one of the pages. Use a hole punch to create the holes. Use your first page as a template to punch holes through all the other pages.

4. Set eyelets in all the holes with an eyelet punch.

5. Bond the iron-on adhesive to your pieces of felt. Copy the templates on pages 122 to 125, and trace the shapes onto the felt with a washable marker or pencil. You can decide how many you want of each shape; for example, four flowers, six cats, etc. Cut out the shapes, remembering to reverse numbers or shapes as necessary.

6. Arrange and bond felt pieces to the pages.

7. Pink all the edges of the pages except for the folded edge.

8. To bind, thread the end of a shoelace through the top and bottom holes of the front cover, pulling the lace flat but not tight. Thread the shoelace ends through each page in sequence. After you add the last page, thread both ends of the shoelace up through the middle hole, knot, and tie in a bow on the front cover.

snuggle
BUNNY

EVERYBODY NEEDS A BUNNY

to love. This colorful, cuddly one is made from terry cloth, so it's soft, washable, and easy to chew on! This appealing toy is destined to be hugged and loved for years to come.

YOU WILL NEED
Patterns on page 119
Pattern paper or graph paper
Pencil
Scissors
Ruler or measuring tape
Velour terry cloth fabric in
   3 different colors, ½ yard
   (45.72 cm) of each
Straight pins
Embroidery thread in 3 different colors
Large-eye needle
Thread in three different colors
Sewing needle
Sewing machine
Polyester fiber stuffing

1. Copy the patterns on page 119 onto pattern paper, adjusting to your desired size and adding a ½-inch (3.8 cm) seam allowance all around. Cut out the patterns.

2. Fold ½ yard (45.72 cm) of the velour terry cloth fabric in the color you want for the bunny's body. Pin the bunny pattern to the fabric and cut out, starting at the fold (you'll have two identical bunny pieces).

3. On the right side of one of the bunny pieces, stitch the nose, lips, and eyes using contrasting colors of embroidery thread and a large-eye needle. Use French knots for the eyes (see page 14), a satin stitch (see page 14) for the nose, and a running stitch (see page 15) for the mouth.

4. Pin the two bunny pieces right sides together. Machine stitch all the way around with a ½-inch (1.3 cm) seam allowance. Leave a 3-inch (7.6 cm) opening on the bunny's side. Clip the curves and turn the bunny right side out, poking the legs, arms, and ears out with a pencil.

5. Stuff the bunny with polyester fiber stuffing, starting at the far end working back to the 3-inch (7.6 cm) hole. Hand stitch closed.

6. Use embroidery thread and a large-eye needle to stitch the fingers and toes.

TO MAKE THE SHIRT

7. Copy the shirt pattern on page 119 onto pattern paper (adjusting to desired size) and cut out. Fold ¼ yard (22.86 cm) of terry cloth in a contrasting color. Pin the shirt pattern to the fabric and cut it out.

8. With the right sides together, machine stitch the shoulder and side seams together with a ½-inch (1.3 cm) seam allowance.

9. Fold under a ½-inch (1.3 cm) hem at the neck and arms. Machine stitch together.

10. Blanket stitch (see page 14) the neck, arms, and bottom.

TO MAKE THE PANTS

11. Copy the pants pattern on page 119, adjusting to desired size. Fold ¼ yard (22.86 cm) of terry cloth fabric in the final color, and pin on the pants pattern. Starting at the fold, cut out the pants.

12. With right sides together, machine stitch the side seams and leg seams together with a ½-inch (1.3 cm) seam allowance.

13. Fold ½ inch (1.3 cm) of the fabric under at the bottom of each pant leg, and hem in place.

14. Blanket stitch around the leg openings with embroidery thread.

WELCOMING BABIES

Why are storks said to deliver babies to expectant parents? Storks are particularly affectionate with their own young, tending to them much longer than other animals do, and this nurturing quality may be a reason they are linked to babies.

Storks portend good luck in European tradition. A stork flying over a home is said to signal an upcoming birth in the house, and if a couple sees a stork when they are together, folk wisdom says that they will soon conceive.

super-absorbent
DIAPER BAG POUCH
DESIGNER: ALLISON SMITH

ANY PARENT CAN TELL YOU *that when you have a baby, you've got a lot of wet stuff. From burp cloths to lotion bottles to wipes, parents are always to be carrying something wet in their diaper bag. This clever envelope-shaped pouch helps keep the moisture away from the other items in the bag. Made from a terry cloth hand towel, it's a simple design with plenty of utility.*

YOU WILL NEED
Terry cloth hand towel
Scissors or rotary tool
Coordinating fabric for trim
Fabric-covered button kit
Measuring tape
Iron
Sewing machine
Straight pins
Sewing needle and thread
Hook-and-loop fastener tape

1. Trim the ends off a hand towel, trimming all the way to the webbing band.

2. Cut the towel in half lengthwise.

3. Using the coordinating fabric, cover the buttons according to package instructions.

4. Make bias tape by cutting two 4 x 48-inch (10.2 cm x 1.2 m) pieces of fabric. Fold in half lengthwise, and press. Fold raw edges into the center (see figures 2 and 3, page 38) and press again.

5. Fold the fabric over one of the short ends of the towel. Cut to fit, and stitch in place on both sides (see figures 2 and 3, page 38). Repeat for the other short edge of the towel.

6. Fold in the finished ends of the towel 5 ½ inches (13.9 cm) on each side, and press. This will create your pockets.

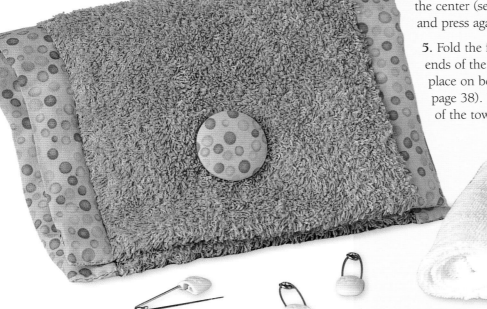

7. Measure in 1 inch (2.5 cm) from each folded end, and position a piece of hook-and-loop fastener tape (sticky side up) parallel to the fold (hook side on one end and loop side on the other). Cut to fit. Stitch into place.

8. Unfold one piece of bias tape and pin it to the long side of the bag. Cut to fit the length. Sew the fabric to the bag along the inside fold line (see figures 2 and 3, page 38).

9. Fold the ends in, and hand stitch in place on each end.

10. Fold the bag in half and hand stitch the button onto the cover.

WELCOMING BABIES

When curious children ask their parents where babies come from, they're often told that babies grow in cabbage patches. This legend may have started in Germany. February was known as "sprout kale" month because it was the month when cabbage was traditionally harvested. It was also the most common month for babies to be born. Cabbage patches also are the frequent haunts of rabbits, known for their prolific procreation—another reason for their association with babies and fertility. In Victorian England, boys were said to have come from the cabbage patch, but girls purportedly sprouted from pink roses.

toile

KEEPSAKE BOX
DESIGNER: ALLISON SMITH

A BABY'S FIRST YEAR *goes by so quickly that it's hard to keep up with all the special moments and milestones. Keeping mementos such as first footprints, the hospital identification bracelet, first photos, and the home-from-the-hospital outfit gives children a wonderful record of their early life. Parents may not have time to make a keepsake box, but they're sure to appreciate this elegant one wrapped in classic toile.*

YOU WILL NEED

Toile fabric in two coordinating
   patterns, approximately
   1 yard (91.4 cm) of each
Measuring tape or ruler
Cardboard box with lid
Scissors
Spray adhesive
Hot glue gun (optional)
Fray retardant
Sewing machine
Pencil or knitting needle
Heavy starch

1. Press and prewash the fabric.

2. Measure the circumference of the box and add 1 inch (2.5 cm). Write down the measurement.

3. Measure the height of the box, multiply by 2, and add 1 inch (2.5 cm). Write down the measurement.

4. Cut a piece of fabric to match your measurements and spread it print-side down on a flat surface.

5. Spray the box with adhesive and place it face up in the center of the fabric. Wrap the side fabric panels around the sides of the box. Turn the excess fabric over the inside edges of the box and smooth it down. Cut the fabric at the corners as necessary.

6. Cut a piece of fabric to fit the inside bottom of the box. Spray the fabric with adhesive and smooth it into place. Cut another piece of fabric to fit the outside bottom of the box as reinforcement. Attach it with hot glue or spray adhesive.

7. To cover the box top, cut one piece of fabric that is large enough to cover the top, the outside edge, and the inside edge of the rim. Place the fabric on a flat surface. Spray the box top with spray adhesive and set it down in the center of the fabric. Smooth and tuck the fabric into place. Cut a piece to cover the inside bottom of the lid, spray the back of it, and smooth it in place.

8. Spray fray retardant on all of the raw edges.

9. For the ties, cut two strips of fabric in the contrasting pattern, each 6 x 48 inches (15.2 x 120 cm). Fold each strip in half length-wise. With right sides together, machine stitch together starting on one short end and stitch down the long side. Turn right side out with the help of a pencil or knitting needle, and press with heavy starch. Hand stitch the second short end closed.

10. Tie the ribbon onto the box.

WELCOMING BABIES

The custom of giving silver spoons to babies seems to have started in Italy, perhaps as early as the 1400s. At a baptism, godparents presented their godchild with a set of 12 silver "apostle spoons." Each spoon featured the symbol of one of the 12 apostles on the upper end of the handle. Few people at the time could afford silver, so giving silver spoons was strictly the province of the rich. To be born "with a silver spoon in one's mouth," which means to be born into wealth, is a common phrase used today that originated from this tradition.

BOOKENDS ARE A MUST

for every nursery. They keep books straight and add a touch of interest to the room. You can make these whimsical bookends with a few simple cuts on a jigsaw. The cute ponies are adapted from a footstool pattern that the designer's father made for him when he was a toddler in the 1950s.

playful pony
BOOKENDS
DESIGNER: TERRY TAYLOR

YOU WILL NEED

Template on page 109

Scissors

4-foot (1.2 m) length of 1 x 12-inch (2.54 x 30.5 cm) wood stock

Ruler or measuring tape

Pencil with eraser

Jigsaw

Medium-grit sandpaper

Wood glue

Power drill

Wood screws

Acrylic paints

Small paintbrush

Black paint pen

Contact cement

Non-slip drawer liner

1. Copy the template on page 109, enlarging it to the size you want, and cut it out.

2. Measure and mark two 5 x 8 ¼-inch (5 x 20.9 cm) rectangles on the wood. Cut them out with the jigsaw.

3. Trace the pony template onto the board you have left. You will need two ponies. Cut them out with the jigsaw.

4. Smooth the edges of each pony with sandpaper.

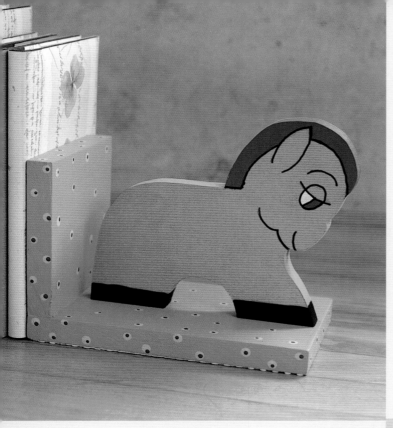

7. Paint the L shapes with two coats of a bright color. Use the eraser of a new pencil as a rubber stamp to make the dots. Dip it in paint and then apply it to the painted surface. Use the handle end of a small paintbrush in the same way to make smaller dots.

8. Position the ponies in the center of the long part of the L shape. Drill wood screws through the bottom of the L into the hooves to attach the pieces. Repeat for the other bookend.

9. Cut two pieces of the drawer liner to cover the bottom of each bookend. Glue the liner to the bottom with contact cement.

5. Paint the ponies with two coats of color. Allow the paint to dry, then paint the mane and eyes. Add the facial details with a paint pen. Paint the hooves as desired. Set the ponies aside.

6. Form an L shape with the rectangles you created in step 2, with the small rectangle on top of the larger one. Run a line of wood glue across the bottom of the smaller rectangle and position it on top of the larger one. Let the glue set for a few hours. Drill two screws through the bottom of the larger rectangle to secure the two pieces. Repeat for the two remaining rectangles.

star attraction
FRAME

THIS GIFT IS A MODERN TWIST *on the classic
silver baby frame. Made with papier mâché and silver
paint, it's an easy project that almost anyone can
make. Considering the many photos parents are
sure to take, a frame is a welcome gift and
this one will complement any nursery décor.*

YOU WILL NEED
Star template on page 121
Scissors
Double-wall cardboard*
Ruler
Pencil
Craft or utility knife
Masking tape (optional)
Cutting mat
Hot glue gun and glue sticks
PVA glue
Jar of water
Small paintbrush
Three polystyrene foam balls,
    each 1 ½ inch (3.8 cm) in diameter
White tissue paper
Thin rope or twine**
Thin wire
Flat container
Plastic sheeting or trash bag
Disposable latex gloves
Gesso or white acrylic paint
Acrylic paint
Metallic acrylic paint

*Use a recycled cardboard box.

**Purchase a suitably sized rope with texture. Look in the rope
and chain area of your local home improvement store.

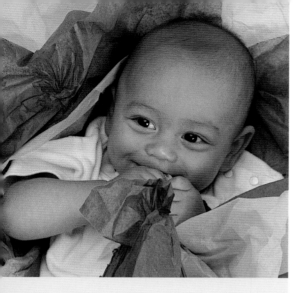

WELCOMING BABIES

The current association between babies and pink and blue seems to have started some time after World War II. Prior to that time, children most commonly wore white with the occasional colored sash for special occasions. White was also used for practical reasons. Natural dyes fade quickly from constant washing, and since children's clothes need frequent laundering, colored clothing was impractical. Babies in many cultures have traditionally worn dark colors like grays, browns, and navy blue for much the same reason.

1. Copy and enlarge the star template on page 121. Cut out the shape. Place the star shape on top of the cardboard (you can tape it down if necessary) and cut around it with a craft knife (use a cutting mat for safety). Repeat for the second piece of cardboard.

2. Mark a circular opening in the center of one cardboard star. The opening is where the photo shows through, so make sure the diameter is wide enough, at least 3 to 4 inches (7.6 to 10.2 cm). Use the craft knife to cut out the circle.

3. Hot glue the two stars together. Brush the surface of the star with the cutout circle with a coat of PVA glue that has been thinned with water. Let it dry at least four hours.

4. Cut the polystyrene balls in half with a craft knife. Hot glue them to the frame as shown in the photo.

5. Tear off tiny strips of tissue paper and wad them into small ball shapes. Hot glue them to the front part of the frame near the polystyrene balls.

6. Hot glue the rope around the edge of the star. To form the little "feet," make a loop and wind a short length of thin wire around the loop. Continue gluing the rope around the frame. Hot glue a length of rope around the circular opening and each of the foam-ball halves.

7. Tear the tissue into 1-inch-wide (2.5 cm) strips. Make a large pile of the strips. Pour PVA glue into a flat container. Thin the glue with an equal amount of water and mix it well. Cover your work area with plastic sheeting. Wearing gloves for easier cleanup, dip strips, one at a time, into the PVA mixture. Cover all sides and edges of the frame with two or three layers of tissue strips. Let them dry flat overnight.

8. Paint the coated star with two coats of gesso or white acrylic paint. Let them dry in between coats.

9. Paint the frame with one or more coats of white or gray acrylic paint. Add metallic paint highlights as desired.

10. To insert a photo, parents should cut the photo to fit the opening and stick it in place with flat tape or nonpermanent glue.

THERE'S NOTHING LIKE FLEECE

to keep a baby warm and cozy when winter comes around. This fleece jumper is simple to make and oh-so-soft and cute. It goes on and comes off easily (a feature parents will love) and can be layered over tights or the pants on page 96 to keep Baby extra toasty.

YOU WILL NEED
Patterns on page 116
Pattern paper or graph paper
½ yard (45.2 cm) of white
  fleece fabric
¼ yard (22.86 cm) of
  purple cotton fabric
Straight pins
Scissors
Iron
Sewing machine
  with buttonholer
½-inch (6 mm)
  bias tape, about
  2 yards (1.8 m)
White thread
Purple thread
Sewing needle
2 wooden buttons

fleecy
JUMPER

1. Copy the patterns on page 116. Enlarge to desired size and copy onto pattern or graph paper. Cut out the patterns.

2. Fold the ½ yard (45.7 cm) of white fleece selvedge to selvedge.

3. Pin the front and back patterns to the fold line. Cut out both pieces.

4. Cut out a 5 x 5-inch (12.7 x 12.7 cm) pocket from the purple fabric. Fold over and press down 1 inch (2.5 cm) of fabric on one side, then fold that piece under ½ inch (1.3 cm) to create a hem for the top of the pocket. Press the other three sides of the pocket under ½ inch (1.3 cm).

5. On the front piece of the jumper, center and pin the pocket and machine stitch in place on the two sides and bottom (the sides you pressed under in step 4).

6. Place the front and back pieces of the jumper right sides together and machine stitch the side seams together with a ½-inch (1.3 cm) seam allowance. Press seams open.

7. Starting at the back center seam of the neck, pin on a strip of bias tape and fold over the edge. Pin the bias tape all the way around the neck and arm openings. Machine stitch in place, joining ends together.

8. With the jumper wrong side out, fold and press a hem 1 ½ inches (3.8 cm) under, then fold under ½ inch (1.3 cm) and press. Machine stitch in place.

9. Hand stitch the buttons in place on the front shoulders.

10. Machine stitch corresponding button-holes on the back shoulders.

fleecy
BABY PANTS

JUST BECAUSE IT'S WINTER *doesn't mean Baby has to stay indoors. Layers of fleece are a perfect solution for winter walks or rides in the stroller. Pair these pants with the fleece jumper on page 95, or they can simply be a gift in themselves. You can make these warm and cozy fleece pants in a matter of hours with a minimum of materials and simple machine sewing skills.*

YOU WILL NEED
Patterns on page 117
Pattern paper or graph paper
Pencil
Scissors
Ruler or measuring tape
½ yard (45.2 cm) of fleece fabric
¼ yard (22.86 cm) of cotton fabric
Straight pins
Sewing machine
Iron
Thread
Sewing needle
2 knit cuffs
1 yard (91.4 cm)
of elastic, ½-inch
(1.3 cm) wide

1. Copy the patterns on page 117. Enlarge to desired size and copy onto pattern or graph paper. Cut out the patterns.

2. Fold the piece of white fleece in half, selvedge to selvedge.

3. Pin the pattern to the fabric and cut it out: you'll need two front pieces, two back pieces, and two gussets (the short edge of the gusset is cut from the fold line).

4. Pin one gusset piece along the center line of the left front, right sides together. Stitch together with a ½-inch (1.3 cm) seam allowance.

5. Repeat for the right front side of the pants.

6. Repeat for the left and right back side of the pants and the second gusset piece.

7. Cut two pocket pieces from the cotton fabric, each 4 ½ x 4 ½ inches (11.4 x 11.4 cm).

8. Press a ½-inch (1.3 cm) hem under on three sides of each pocket piece. Press 1 inch (2.5 cm) over on the remaining side, then fold ½-inch (1.3 cm) under again and hem. Repeat for the remaining pocket piece.

9. Place the pockets in position on the front of the pants. Machine stitch in place along three sides, leaving the top open.

10. With right sides together, pin the front and back pieces together. Machine stitch the side seams and inseam with a ½-inch (1.3 cm) seam allowance. Press seams open.

11. Machine baste the bottom of the leg openings. Pull the thread, gathering the leg opening to fit the cuffs.

12. With the pants wrong side out, pin the cuffs and the raw edges of the leg openings together. Machine stitch the cuffs to the openings.

13. Turn under a 1-inch (2.5 cm) waistband and press a ¼-inch (6 mm) hem under it. Machine stitch around the waist, leaving a 3-inch (7.6 cm) opening in the back.

14. Thread the elastic through the waistband. At the place where the ends meet, machine stitch together. Hand stitch the 3-inch (7.6 cm) opening closed.

WELCOMING BABIES

The Chinese version of the stork is the celestial fairy. The fairy is said to ride around the world on a unicorn delivering babies.

the hub of activity in any nursery. Parents need so many items, such as diapers, wipes, lotions, and powders—it's easy for clutter to build up. This charming organizer saves space and keeps useful items close at hand. The sewing is simple, but the construction is sturdy. Later, when Baby is older, it can be used on a bedpost to stash toys.

YOU WILL NEED
1 yard (91.44 cm) background fabric
1 yard (91.44 cm) pocket fabric
Scissors
1 piece of fusible interfacing, 11 x 28 inches (27.9 x 71.1 cm)
Sewing machine
Coordinating thread
Iron
Straight pins
Pencil or knitting needle
Sewing needle

changing table
POCKET ORGANIZER
DESIGNER: JOAN MORRIS

1. Prewash both fabrics.

2. Cut two pieces of background fabric, each 11 x 28 inches (27.9 x 71.1 cm). Cut a piece of pocket fabric, 9 x 34 inches (22.9 x cm). Cut another piece of fabric to the same dimensions—you can use the background fabric or pocket fabric for this piece. Cut eight strips of pocket fabric, each 2 x 18 inches (5.2 x 47 cm).

3. Attach a piece of fusible webbing to the wrong side of one of the pieces of background fabric, following manufacturer's instructions.

4. Place two 9 x 34-inch (22.9 x 86.36 cm) pieces right sides together and machine stitch together along one long edge with a ½-inch (1.3 cm) seam allowance. Fold the wrong sides together and press the edges.

5. To make pleats for the pockets, measure in 1 ½ inches (3.8 cm) from the left short edge. Measure and fold the fabric back 1 ½ inches (3.8 cm) to the right. Measure ½ inch (1.3 cm) back from the first fold line, and fold under, creating a valley fold in the middle of your first fold (see figure 1). Pin the pleat in place.

FIGURE I

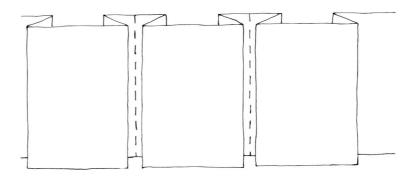

WELCOMING BABIES

In Australian Aboriginal tradition, members of a new baby's community "smoke" a baby as a gesture of purification. A fire of konkerberry wood is built and water is dripped over it to dampen the flame. Fragrant leaves are dropped in the fire to create smoke. Water is lightly sprayed on the baby's head, chest, back, and legs, and he is then briefly held in the aromatic smoke. The fragrance is thought to cleanse the baby so that he gets off to a good start in life.

6. Measure 9 inches (22.9 cm) to the left of the fold line you created in step 5 to create your next fold line. Measure over 1 inch (2.5 cm) to the left of that mark and fold over to meet the other mark. Pin the pleat in place, then stitch.

7. Repeat steps 5 and 6 for the additional pockets.

8. Machine baste the short edges and bottom long edge of the pocket piece to the fused piece of the background material, leaving the top long edge open to form the pockets.

9. Machine stitch the center of two pleats onto the background fabric, being careful not to catch pleats. Repeat on the other pleats.

10. Fold each of the 2 x 18-inch (5.2 x 45.7 cm) strips in half lengthwise with right sides together. Machine stitch across the short edge with a ¼-inch (6mm) seam allowance, then down the length leaving one end open. Turn rights side out with a pencil or knitting needle. Press flat.

11. Line up the raw edges of two of the tie pieces to the top of the front piece of background fabric, 1 inch (2.5 cm) from the right edge. Repeat with two ties 1 inch (2.5 cm) in from the left, then over the two center folds. Machine stitch in place.

12. Pin the second piece of background fabric, right sides together with the pocketed piece. Be sure the ties are loose between the two pieces, not caught in the seams. Stitch around all the edges, leaving 6 inches (15.2 cm) open at the bottom.

13. Cut the corners diagonally, turn right side out, and press.

14. Hand stitch closed.

little things within arms' reach when they're at the changing table, and a dozen little things can make a mess. This cute tray will keep things straight and complement any nursery décor. Inexpensive tin containers can be found at discount stores and easily transformed with paint and buttons.

YOU WILL NEED

Tin containers
Ruler or measuring tape
Sturdy cardboard
Pencil or marker
Craft knife
Masking tape
Blue gingham fabric
Scissors
Liquid starch
Spray adhesive
Metal primer
Paintbrush
White spray paint
Blue craft paint
White craft paint
Jar of water
Paper towels
Blue thread
Needle
White buttons
Hot glue gun and glue sticks

cute-as-a-button
CHANGING TABLE TRAY
DESIGNER: ALLISON SMITH

1. Measure the dimensions of the containers that you plan to use. Add 1 inch (2.5 cm) to the length and ¾ inch (1.9 cm) to the depth.

2. Measure and mark a piece of cardboard to match figure 1 (see page 102). Your measurements will vary depending on the size of the containers. Cut the cardboard to size with a craft knife.

3. Fold up the flaps of the cardboard and secure with masking tape.

4. Cut a piece of gingham that generously covers the inside of the tray, with enough extra to wrap around the outside edges and fold under. Soak the fabric in liquid starch. Squeeze the excess starch out of the fabric.

5. Working from the inside, spread the fabric over the tray, smoothing out the wrinkles as you go. Fold and tuck the fabric to neatly cover the tray, trimming excess fabric when necessary. Allow to dry.

6. Cut a second small rectangle of fabric to fit the bottom outside of the tray. Spray the fabric with adhesive and smooth onto the bottom of the tray.

7. Paint the tins with the metal primer. Allow to dry.

8. Paint the inside of the tins with the white spray paint. Allow to dry.

9. Paint the outside of the tins with two coats of blue paint. Allow to dry.

10. Dilute the white craft paint by half. Paint over the blue paint, and then immediately wipe off with paper towels, leaving a milky, distressed finish.

11. Use the needle and thread to sew up the holes of the button. Attach the buttons to the containers with hot glue.

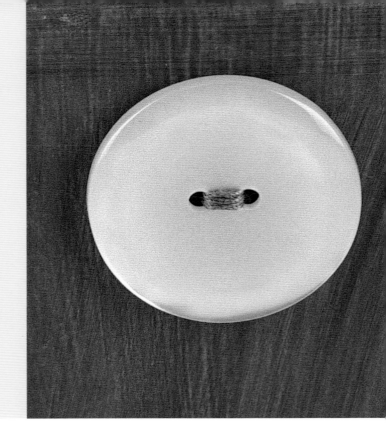

FIGURE I

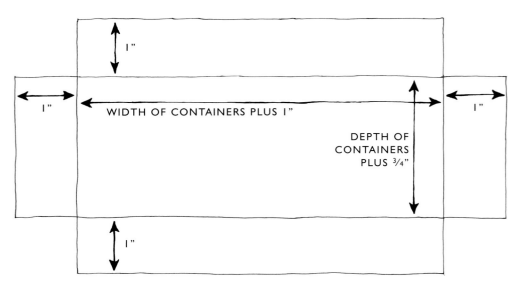

little bird

BABY ALBUM
DESIGNER: GWEN DIEHN

A LITTLE FOOT, A LITTLE HAND, *a sweet sleepy smile—there are so many images of babies that parents want to capture. This sweet album is perfect for keeping and displaying Baby's photos, cards, and other keepsakes. To create the covers, you'll use simple bookbinding and collage techniques as well as your own imagination. The little bird on this album was created with a hand-carved rubber stamp, but you can find beautiful commercial stamps to use as well. The small size makes it convenient to carry as a brag book—a great gift for grandparents too.*

2 pieces of Davey board* (medium thickness), 5 x 8 inches (12.7 x 20.3 cm) each

Mat knife

Metal ruler

Emery board or small piece of sandpaper

Bone folder

Scissors

20 to 30 pieces of medium-weight paper for pages, cut to 4 ⅞ x 9 ¼ inches (12.4 x 23.5 cm)

Decorative papers for collage and end papers**

Cutting mat or piece of cardboard

PVA glue

Craft brush

Eraser carving material or commercial rubber stamp (optional)

Stamp pad (optional)

Polymer or acrylic varnish, mat, or satin finish

Soft brush for varnish

2 yards (1.82 m) of ribbon

10 small grommets (optional)

Grommet-setting tool and hammer (optional)

Large-eye sewing needle

Scrap paper

Small jar or water

Rags

Power drill with ⅛-inch (3 mm) drill bit

Graphite pencil

Scrap wood (to put under album while drilling)

2 bulldog clips

*archival board available at art supply stores

**The first layer of paper on the covers should be a fairly neutral paper, such as a solid color.

1. Measure and cut the two Davey board covers with a ruler and mat knife. Be sure the grain of the board is going parallel to the spine (the 5-inch [12.7 cm] edge). To determine the grain, flex the board-the grain goes in the direction that flexes more easily. Use a bone folder to smooth out edges. If any edges are ragged from cutting, lightly sand them with an emery board or sandpaper.

2. Tear or cut as many pages as you want to have in the album (you can easily add more later). The pages should be about ⅛ inch (3 mm) shorter than the height of the cover boards and about 1 ¼ inches (3.2 cm) longer than the length of the covers to accommodate for the binding.

3. Cut two pieces of neutral decorative paper to about 1 inch (2.5 cm) larger than the cover board (in this case, 6 x 9 inches [15.2 x 22.9 cm]). These pieces will wrap around your front and back covers.

4. Place the board you'll use for the front cover on a cutting mat or piece of cardboard. Measure a strip 1 ¼ inches (3.2 cm) in from the left edge (see figure 1). Use the ruler and mat knife to cut off this strip. Put aside this strip for later use.

5. Cut another strip ¼ inch (6 mm) in from the edge that you just cut (see figure 2).

6. Brush glue all over the decorative paper that you'll use to wrap the front cover. While the glue is still wet, carefully place the 1 ¼-inch (3.2 cm) strip along the left side the paper. Leave a ¼-inch (3 mm) gap, and place the remaining piece of board on the paper (see figure 3).

7. Bend down each corner of the decorative paper over the edges of the board (see figure 4), smoothing in place with a bone folder.

8. Add a little glue to each of the side flaps, then fold them over and smooth them in place with a bone folder (see figure 5).

FIGURE 1

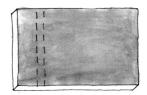

FIGURE 2

FIGURE 3

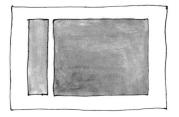

FIGURE 4

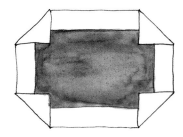

FIGURE 5

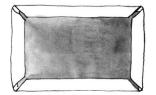

9. Repeat steps 7 and 8 for the back cover—this piece of board is still intact, since you didn't cut the 1 ¼-inch (3.2 cm) strip from it (see figure 6).

10. Make a collage on each cover board by gluing on strips of paper in a design of your choice. If you want to add rubber-stamped images, carve them with the mat knife and eraser carving material, or use commercial stamps. When you have finished both cover collages, brush varnish over the outside to protect the delicate papers.

11. Measure, and then cut or tear decorative papers for end pages inside each cover. Each page should be about ⅛ inch (3 mm) shorter and narrower than the cover width and length. Brush PVA all over the back of the covers, and press the end papers in place (see figure 7).

12. Measure and fold a 1 ¼-inch (3.2 cm) strip along the left side edge of each text page (see figure 8). The flap that you create will be a spine thickener, and will keep the fore edge (opposite edge) of the album from splaying when you add photographs or other elements to the pages.

13. Stack the folded text pages with the folded piece to the left of each page. Align the text pages inside the covers. Fold a piece of scrap paper over the top and bottom edge of the album to protect the covers from the bulldog clips. Without moving the covers or text pages, clip the album together (see figure 9).

14. Mark holes along the left front cover in the spine area (the small strip). The holes should be about 1 inch (2.5 cm) apart and at least ½ inch (1.3 cm) in from the edge. Keeping the bulldog clips in place, place the album on top of a piece of scrap wood, and use a drill with a ⅛-inch (3 mm) drill bit to drill holes through both covers and all text pages at once.

FIGURE 6

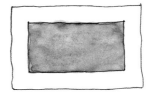

FIGURE 7

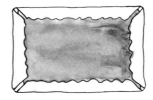

FIGURE 8

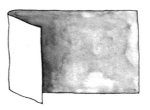

FIGURE 9

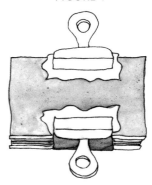

FIGURE 10

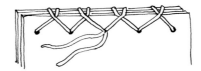

15. If you will be using grommets to finish the holes, place a grommet in each hole and set it with a grommet-setting tool and hammer. Turn the album over, and set grommets in the holes on the back cover.

16. Keeping the clips in place, thread a needle with 2 yards (1.82 m) of thin ribbon. Do not tie a knot. Put the needle into the hole where you want the ribbon to tie. In the example, the needle was first placed in the middle hole, from the front side of the cover.

15. Wrap the ribbon around the spine and go into the next hole up, entering the hole from the front of the album. Keep the ribbon flat to avoid twisting. Continue wrapping up the spine and entering the next hole up until you come to the top of the album, then start back down the spine by wrapping the spine and putting the needle in the first hole down from the top, working always from the front of the album. Continue in this manner until you reach the bottom of the album. At the bottom, start back up toward the middle, wrapping and putting the needle into the next hole up. When you come to the hole just below the middle hole, tie the ribbon in a single knot, and then at the middle hole, tie a bow (see figure 10).

template
ROYAL TREATMENT WASHCLOTH
PAGE 29

ENLARGE TO DESIRED SIZE

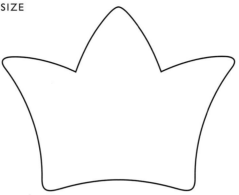

template
STAR BRIGHT APPLIQUÉ
PAGE 32

ENLARGE TO DESIRED SIZE

template

PLAYFUL PONY BOOKENDS

PAGE 91

ENLARGE TO DESIRED SIZE

template
BABY PIXIE HAT
PAGE 72

ENLARGE TO DESIRED SIZE

template
TWINKLY STAR TOY
PAGE 40

ENLARGE 200%

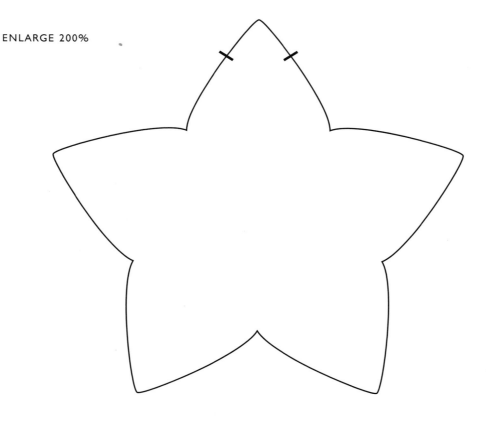

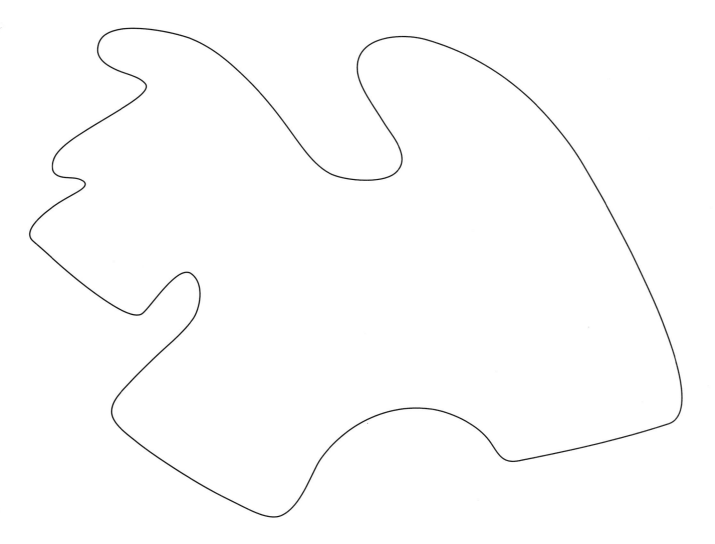

ENLARGE TO DESIRED SIZE

GOOD LITTLE EATER OILCLOTH BIB

PAGE 50

ENLARGE TO DESIRED SIZE

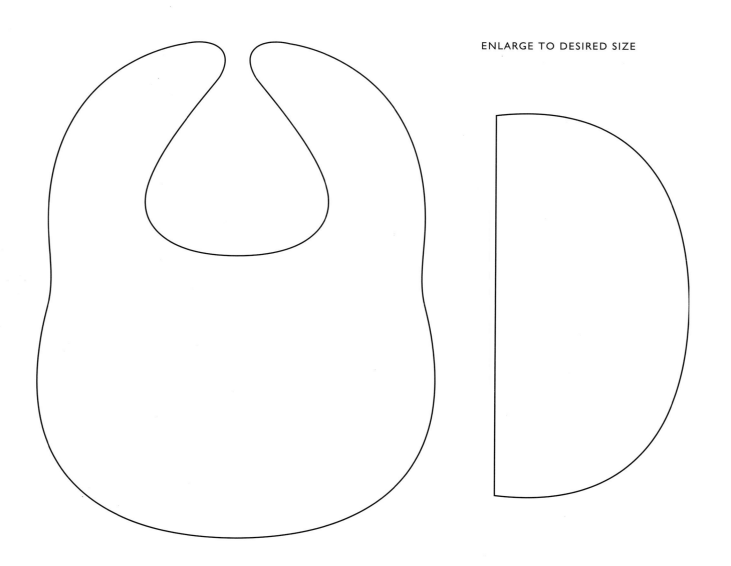

BIG, FUN SOFT BABY BLOCKS AND BALLS
PAGE 24

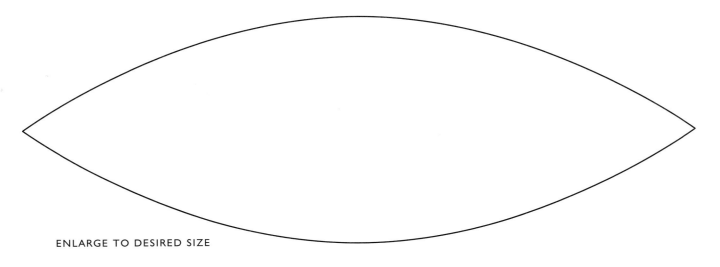

ENLARGE TO DESIRED SIZE

COLOR-SLICE FELT RATTLE
PAGE 57

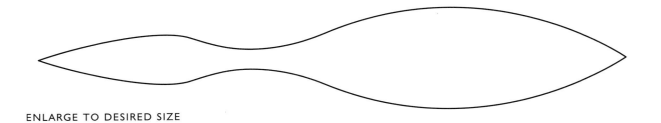

ENLARGE TO DESIRED SIZE

NURSING AND PLAY PILLOW

PAGE 61

ENLARGE TO DESIRED SIZE

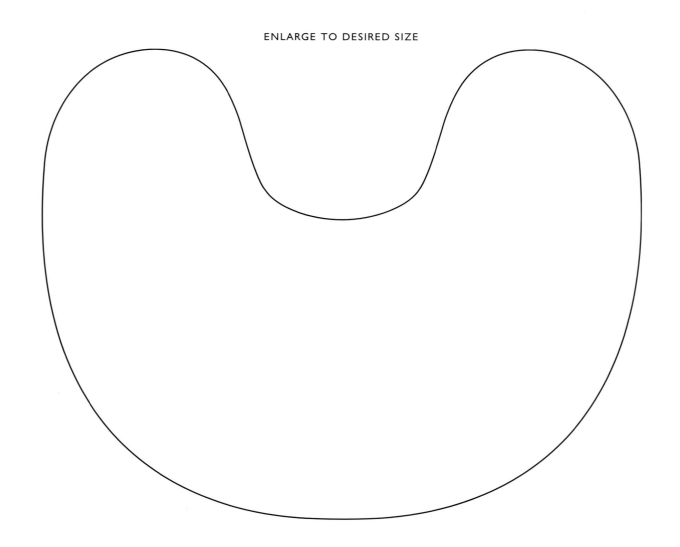

LITTLE LADYBUG SUNHAT

PAGE 68

ENLARGE TO DESIRED SIZE

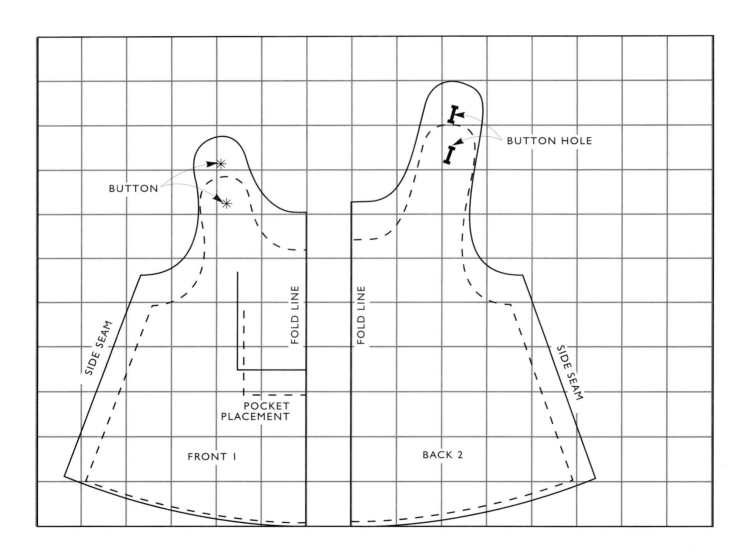

BUTTON HOLE

BUTTON

SIDE SEAM

FOLD LINE

POCKET PLACEMENT

FRONT 1

FOLD LINE

SIDE SEAM

BACK 2

FLEECY PANTS

PAGE 96

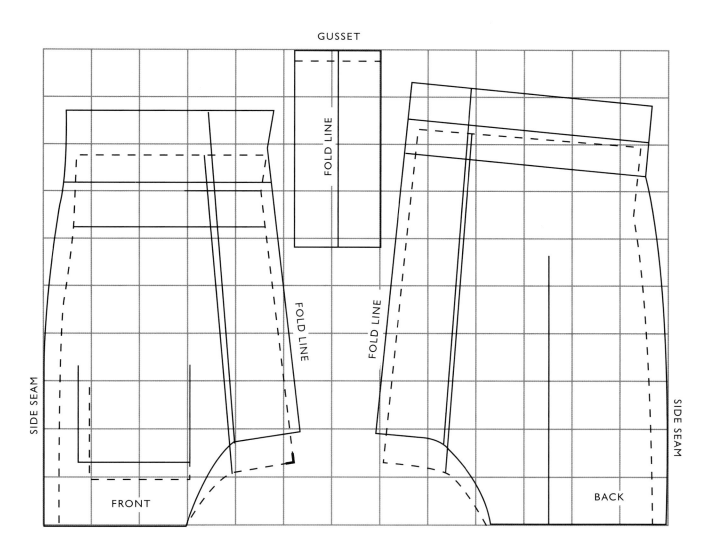

GUSSET

FOLD LINE

FOLD LINE

FOLD LINE

SIDE SEAM

SIDE SEAM

FRONT

BACK

FAIRYTALE TREASURE CHEST

PAGE 79

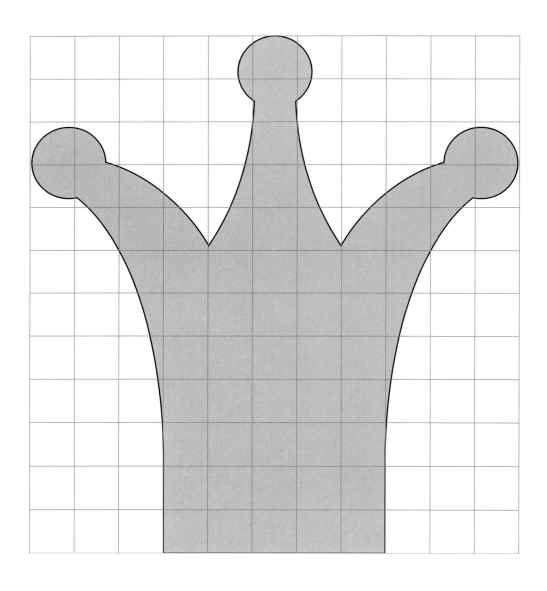

template

SNUGGLE BUNNY
PAGE 82

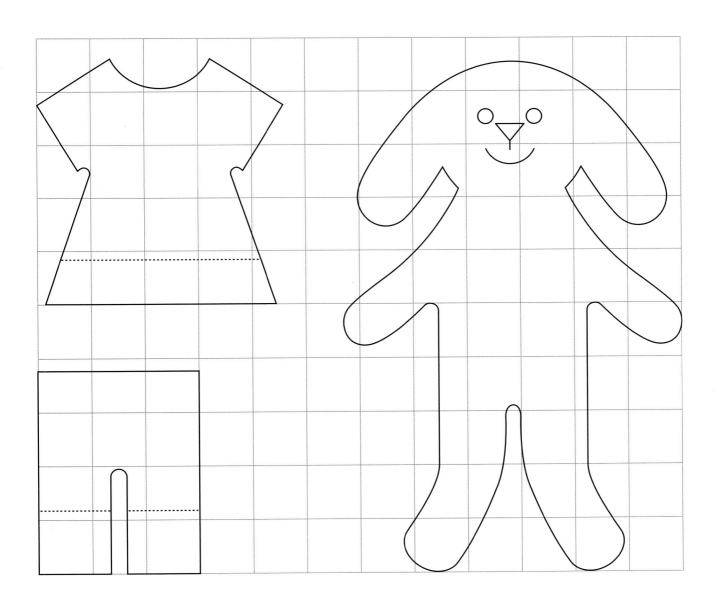

template

HEART-FELT BOOTIES

PAGE 24

ENLARGE TO DESIRED SIZE

template

SWEET LITTLE SOCKS

PAGE 53

ENLARGE TO DESIRED SIZE

template

STAR ATTRACTION FRAME

PAGE 93

ENLARGE TO DESIRED SIZE

BABY'S FIRST COUNTING BOOK
PAGE 80

ENLARGE TO DESIRED SIZE

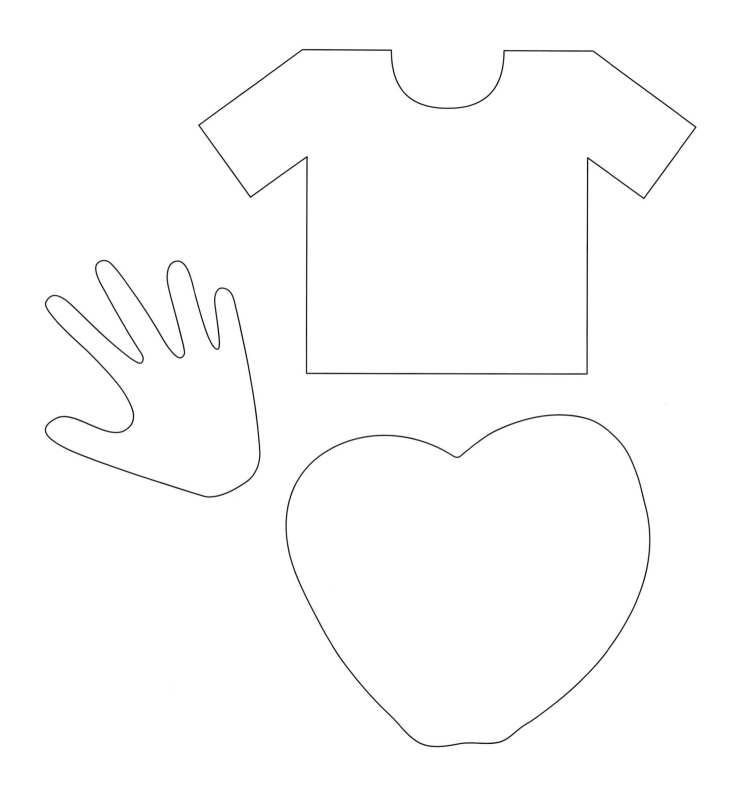

ACKNOWLEDGMENTS

Kudos and thanks to all the talented designers who created such adorable projects for the book. A special nod to Terry Taylor and Joan Morris for all their help with project instructions, sewing tutorials, and "translations." Praise and gratitude to our art director Stacey Budge, whose incredible talent, energy, vision, and impeccable organization made the photo shoot run so smoothly and made the book beautiful. Thanks also to Sandra Stambaugh for her usual high caliber of photography and wonderful way with babies. Shannon Yokeley deserves special thanks for her photo shoot assistance, too. To all the parents of the babies, thanks for allowing us to grace the pages with all of their beautiful faces. Our baby models were: Jude Seo, Jackson Chase, Elijah Clinkscales-King, Dylan Turner Ramsey, Kaegon Matlock, Aurora Moon, Jaylan Pickens, Mina Walker, Maxwell Butterworth, Madeline Ayling, Jayhawk Julian, Sam Knight, Grace O'Connor, and of course Maeve Goldberg, my own beautiful daughter. Special thanks to Wayne and Lisa Forehand for lending us Rachael's cherubic face for the cover, and to Maria Luisa for her excellent coaching. Speaking of the cover, thanks to Barbara Zaretsky for her expert design and John Widman for his professionalism and gorgeous photography.

CONTRIBUTING DESIGNERS

Gwen Diehn teaches art and book arts at Warren Wilson College near Asheville, North Carolina. She is the author of several Lark Books, including *Making Books That Fly, Fold, Wrap, Hide, Pop Up, Twist, and Turn: Books for Kids to Make* (1998); and *Simple Printmaking* (2001).

Miegan Gordon is an artist who works freelance from her home in Asheville, North Carolina.

Joan K. Morris' artistic endeavors have led her down many successful creative paths. A childhood interest in sewing turned into professional costuming for motion pictures. After studying ceramics, Joan ran her own clay wind chime business for 15 years. Since 1993, Joan's Asheville, North Carolina coffee house, Vincent's Ear, has provided a vital meeting place for all varieties of artists and thinkers.